FROM CONVERSATION TO COURTROOM

ELEVATING CLIENT ENGAGEMENT AND STRATEGIC ADVOCACY

DHHRITI ARORRA & DEVYANSH ARORA

Made with ♥ on the Notion Press Platform
www.notionpress.com

In the delicate dance of advocacy, the lawyer's words are not merely tools of persuasion but instruments of justice, shaping the truth that bridges conversations and verdicts

Contents

Foreword

In every profession, foundational skills define success, and in the legal field, few are more crucial than the art of advocacy. As a lawyer, I have seen firsthand how the power of words and the nuances of communication can shape outcomes—whether in delicate client interviews, critical negotiations, or before a judge in court. From Conversation to Courtroom is born out of this understanding: at the heart of legal practice lies the ability to counsel, argue, and persuade with clarity, precision, and ethical integrity.

This book is not merely a guide for young lawyers learning the ropes or seasoned practitioners honing their skills; it is a comprehensive exploration of the tools that define effective legal advocacy. From mastering oral arguments to drafting precise legal documents, from building meaningful client relationships to upholding the highest standards of professional conduct, this work draws on my experiences, lessons, and insights into what it takes to excel in our profession.

What is unique about the legal profession is its demand for both intellectual rigour and emotional intelligence. The ability to craft compelling arguments is only as strong as listening, empathising, and understanding the people we serve. As you read through the pages of this book, you will discover that successful advocacy is not just about the technicalities of law; it's about bridging the human elements of communication with the structured nature of legal reasoning.

I hope this book provides readers with both practical skills and thoughtful perspectives, allowing them to engage in advocacy that is effective and profoundly aligned with the ethical standards our profession upholds. Whether you are stepping into a courtroom for the first time or are a veteran practitioner, I trust that this book will offer you valuable insights into the art of advocacy.

The journey from conversation to courtroom is filled with complexity, challenges, and opportunities. I sincerely hope this work serves as a companion and guide for those walking that path—arming them with the skills, knowledge, and integrity needed to advocate for justice and truth.

Preface

As a law student, I have always been fascinated by the intersection between communication and law practice. In my journey, I have realised that while legal knowledge is undoubtedly crucial, the ability to advocate effectively—to speak, listen, and argue with clarity and purpose—defines a successful lawyer. From Conversation to Courtroom is an exploration of these advocacy skills, shaped by my experiences and studies, and aimed at equipping others like me with the tools necessary to thrive in the legal profession.

Throughout my academic journey, I have encountered countless situations where clear communication made all the difference—whether in a classroom discussion, a moot court, or peer-to-peer debates. Yet, the art of advocacy extends far beyond the classroom. It encompasses the delicate balance of persuasion and professionalism, empathy and logic, all within the framework of ethical conduct. This book seeks to bridge the gap between theory and practice, guiding readers from the foundational aspects of client interviews and counselling to the complex dynamics of courtroom advocacy.

Law students are taught to analyse cases, dissect statutes, and craft legal arguments. But often, the importance of presenting our thoughts—how we connect with clients, judges, and opposing counsel—can be overlooked. This book aims to fill that gap, providing practical tips on legal communication and emphasising the ethical standards that underpin every successful legal practice.

In writing this book, I have drawn inspiration from my own experiences, the lessons imparted by professors and mentors, and the many challenges and opportunities that come with being a law student. I have structured this work to serve fellow law students and young legal professionals navigating the early stages of their careers. The goal is to provide a comprehensive guide to mastering the various forms of advocacy, from the quiet conversations with clients to the powerful arguments made in court.

As you read through these chapters, I hope you find insights that enhance your legal skills and inspire you to approach the profession with purpose and integrity. The journey from conversation to courtroom is one of constant learning and growth, and I am excited to share this exploration with you.

Devyansh Arora

Acknowledgements

Writing From Conversation to Courtroom has been a journey of learning, reflection, and growth, and I am deeply grateful to those who have supported me along the way.

First and foremost, I would like to thank my family for their unwavering belief in me. To my parents, your encouragement and constant support have been my driving force. To my mentors and professors, your guidance has shaped my understanding of the law and my appreciation for the art of advocacy. Your insights and teaching have inspired much of what this book explores, and I am incredibly fortunate to have learned from you.

I am also grateful to my friends and peers who have been sounding boards, critics, and companions throughout this process. The discussions, debates, and collaborations with all of you have enriched my perspective and pushed me to think critically about the many facets of legal practice.

Your influence has been invaluable to the legal community and the institutions that have provided me with opportunities to learn and grow. From the classroom to the moot court and beyond, these experiences have shaped my understanding of being an advocate.

Finally, I would like to thank all who have engaged with this work. Whether you are a fellow student, a young professional, or an experienced lawyer, I hope this book provides valuable insights supporting your legal journey.

From Conversation to Courtroom is a product of collaboration, learning, and perseverance, and I sincerely appreciate everyone who has played a role in its creation.

Devyansh Arora

CHAPTER ONE

ADVOCACY SKILLS FOR LAWYERS: DO'S AND DON'TS IN PROFESSIONAL CONDUCT

-Dhhriti Arorra

Abstract

This research paper explores the essential advocacy skills for lawyers, focusing on the dos and don'ts of professional conduct. It examines the foundational elements of advocacy, including legal knowledge and research, communication skills, and ethical conduct. The paper delves into the skills required for effective advocacy, such as preparation and organisation, persuasion and argumentation, and building relationships. It also highlights the ethical considerations that lawyers must adhere to, including avoiding conflicts of interest, maintaining confidentiality, and refraining from misrepresentations. By understanding these principles, lawyers can enhance their effectiveness, maintain ethical standards, and ultimately serve the best interests of their clients.

OVERVIEW

Advocacy, the art of presenting and defending a cause or argument, is a cornerstone of the legal profession. It demands a delicate balance of legal knowledge, communication skills, and ethical conduct. Effective advocacy is essential for ensuring that clients' rights are protected, justice is served, and the rule of law is upheld.

This research paper delves into the essential advocacy skills for lawyers, exploring the dos and don'ts that shape professional conduct. By understanding these principles, lawyers can enhance their effectiveness, maintain ethical standards, and ultimately serve the best interests of their clients.

The paper is divided into three main parts:

- **The Foundation of Advocacy:** This section explores the fundamental skills and knowledge essential for effective advocacy, including legal expertise and research, communication skills, and ethical conduct.
- **The Dos of Advocacy:** This section highlights the specific practices and techniques that lawyers should adopt to enhance their advocacy skills, such as preparation and organisation, persuasion and argumentation, and building relationships.

- **The Don'ts of Advocacy:** This section discusses the pitfalls and mistakes that lawyers should avoid, such as ethical violations, poor communication, and inadequate preparation.

This paper examines these three aspects of advocacy to provide a comprehensive overview of the skills and practices that lawyers must master to succeed in their profession.

PART I: THE FOUNDATION OF ADVOCACY

Legal Knowledge and Research Thorough Understanding

A deep understanding of relevant legal principles, statutes, and case law is fundamental for effective advocacy. This requires a comprehensive grasp of:

- **Substantive Law:** A thorough understanding of the specific legal principles that govern the area of law relevant to the case. This includes knowledge of statutes, case law, and legal doctrines. For example, a lawyer representing a client accused of driving under the influence would need to understand the rules governing DUI in their jurisdiction, including the elements of the crime, the penalties, and any potential defences.
- **Procedural Law:** A familiarity with the rules and procedures that govern legal proceedings. This includes knowledge of court procedures, rules of evidence, and other procedural matters. For example, a lawyer preparing for a trial must understand the rules of

evidence, the order of proof, and the proper procedures for objecting to evidence.

- **Jurisdictional Differences:** Lawyers who practice in multiple jurisdictions or handle cases with interstate or international implications should be aware of the differences in legal principles and procedures between them.

Effective Research

The ability to conduct comprehensive legal research is essential for effective advocacy. This involves knowing where to find the relevant legal authorities, such as statutes, case law, and legal treatises. This may include using legal databases, law libraries, and online resources. Familiarity with legal databases, such as LexisNexis, Westlaw, and Google Scholar, is essential for efficient legal research. These databases allow lawyers to search for specific legal terms and retrieve relevant cases, statutes, and other legal materials. It is knowing how to cite legal authorities in legal documents properly. This includes understanding the different citation styles (e.g., Bluebook, ALWD) and the rules for citing cases, statutes, and other legal materials. The ability to critically analyse legal materials and extract relevant information. This involves understanding the legal principles and reasoning underlying court decisions and statutory provisions.

Staying Updated

The legal landscape is constantly evolving, with new laws being enacted, court decisions being issued, and legal trends emerging. Lawyers need to stay updated on these developments to provide effective representation. This involves keeping track of new legislation, court decisions, and other relevant legal developments in their practice area. This can be done through subscribing to legal newsletters, attending legal conferences, and reading legal journals. They are participating in continuing education courses to enhance their legal knowledge and skills. This may include attending CLE seminars, taking online courses, or pursuing advanced law degrees. Building relationships with other lawyers in their practice area can provide valuable insights into legal developments and best practices. Lawyers can provide their clients with the highest legal representation by thoroughly understanding the law, conducting effective research, and staying updated on legal developments.

COMMUNICATION SKILLS

Oral Advocacy

Oral advocacy is the art of presenting and defending arguments orally in court, at hearings, or in negotiations. Effective oral advocacy requires articulating complex legal concepts clearly and understandably. This involves using plain language, avoiding legal jargon, and structuring arguments logically and persuasively. Confidence and poise when speaking in public. This includes maintaining eye contact, speaking clearly and loudly, and using appropriate body language. The ability to use persuasive techniques, such as rhetorical devices, appeal to emotions and use evidence effectively. The ability to ask relevant and probing questions to elicit information from witnesses, opposing counsel, and the court. This includes knowing how to frame questions in a leading or non-leading way and how to object to improper questions.

Written Advocacy

Written advocacy involves the preparation of legal documents, such as briefs, memos, and contracts. Effective written advocacy requires writing concisely and persuasively. This consists of using plain language, avoiding legal jargon, and organising ideas logically and coherently—familiarity with the conventions of legal writing, including proper citation format, grammar, and punctuation. Careful attention to detail is essential for ensuring that legal documents are accurate and error-free—the ability to present arguments persuasively, using evidence and legal reasoning to support the client's position.

Active Listening

Active listening is paying attention to what others say, understanding their perspective, and responding appropriately. This is essential for effective communication with clients, witnesses, and opposing counsel. Active listening involves maintaining eye contact with the speaker, showing that you are engaged and attentive. They are allowing the speaker to finish speaking without interrupting. Ask questions to ensure that you understand what the speaker is saying, and restate what the speaker has said in your own words to show that you appreciate their perspective —showing empathy and understanding for the speaker's feelings and experiences. Practical communication skills are essential for successful advocacy. By developing strong oral and written communication skills and practising active listening, lawyers can enhance their ability to represent their clients effectively and build relationships with others in the legal profession.

Ethical Conduct in Advocacy

Ethical conduct is a cornerstone of the legal profession. It is essential for maintaining public trust in the justice system and ensuring that lawyers act in the best interests of their clients. Lawyers are bound by professional codes of conduct that outline the ethical standards they must adhere to.

Key Ethical Principles:

- **Confidentiality:** Lawyers must maintain the confidentiality of their client's information. This includes protecting client secrets, privileged communications, and any information that could harm the client.
- **Truthfulness:** Lawyers must be truthful in dealing with clients, courts, and opposing counsel. This includes avoiding misrepresentations, making false or misleading statements, and ensuring their arguments are based on accurate information.
- **Competence:** Lawyers must be competent in their practice area. This means having the knowledge, skills,

and training to represent their clients effectively.

- **Diligence:** Lawyers must be diligent in their representation of clients. This means acting promptly, efficiently, and effectively to protect clients' interests.
- **Avoidance of Conflicts of Interest:** Lawyers must avoid conflicts of interest that could compromise their duties to their clients. This includes situations where a lawyer has a personal interest that could interfere with their client's representation.
- **Fairness to Opposing Party and the Court:** Lawyers must treat opposing counsel and the court respectfully. This includes avoiding abusive tactics, ensuring that discovery is conducted fairly, and complying with court orders.
- **Pro Bono Service:** Lawyers are responsible for providing pro bono service to those who cannot afford legal representation. This helps to ensure that everyone has access to justice.

Ethical Dilemmas

Lawyers often face ethical dilemmas where they must weigh competing interests or make difficult choices. Some common ethical dilemmas include:

Confidentiality vs. Duty to Report: In some cases, lawyers may have a duty to report illegal or harmful conduct, even if it violates client confidentiality.

Conflicts of Interest: Lawyers may have conflicts of interest that could affect their representation of a client.

Zealous Advocacy vs. Fairness: Lawyers must be zealous advocates for their clients and act fairly and ethically. Striking this balance can sometimes be difficult.

Ethical Decision-Making

When faced with an ethical dilemma, lawyers should follow a systematic approach to decision-making. This approach typically involves:

- **Identifying the ethical issue:** Clearly define the moral dilemma and the relevant ethical principles.
- **Gathering information:** Gather all relevant information about the situation, including the facts, the law, and the potential consequences of different actions.
- **Considering alternatives:** Explore the possible options and their potential consequences.
- **Consulting with others:** Seek advice from colleagues, mentors, or ethics committees.
- **Making a decision:** Make a decision based on the ethical principles and your analysis of the situation.

Ethical conduct is essential for the legal profession. Lawyers can maintain public trust and ensure they act in their client's best interests by adhering to the moral principles outlined in the professional codes of conduct.

PART II: THE DOS OF ADVOCACY

Preparation And Organization Case Analysis

Identifying Key Issues is very important. The first step in preparing a case is identifying the critical legal and factual issues. This involves carefully reviewing the pleadings, evidence, and applicable law to determine the core disputes that must be resolved. Understanding the client's goals and objectives for the case is also essential. This will help the lawyer tailor their strategy to meet the client's needs and expectations. A theory of the case is a concise statement that explains the client's version of events and the legal basis for their claims. This helps to focus the lawyer's efforts and guide the development of the case strategy.

Evidence Gathering

Once the key issues have been identified, the lawyer must gather all relevant evidence to support the client's claims. This may include documents, witness statements, expert testimony, and physical evidence. It is essential to preserve evidence to ensure that it can be used at trial or in other legal proceedings. This may involve protecting documents, securing witness testimony, or maintaining physical evidence. Evidence should be organised in a way that is easy to access and understand. This may involve creating a timeline of events, categorising evidence by type, or using electronic tools to organise and manage evidence.

Presentation Preparation

A well-structured presentation is essential for effectively communicating the client's case. The presentation should have a clear introduction, body, and conclusion. Visual aids, such as charts, graphs, and photographs, can help clarify complex information and make a presentation more engaging. Rehearsing the presentation in advance can help the lawyer to become more comfortable with the material and identify any areas that need improvement. The lawyer should anticipate questions from the judge, jury, or opposing counsel and prepare answers.

By following these steps, lawyers can ensure they are well-prepared to present their client's case and maximise their chances of success.

Persuasion And Argumentation

Clear And Concise Arguments

Arguments should be presented clearly and logically, each point building upon the previous one. This helps to ensure that the argument is easy to follow and understand. While legal knowledge is essential, using excessive legal jargon can confuse the audience. Lawyers should strive to explain complex legal concepts in plain language that is easy to understand. Strong language can emphasise key points and make the argument more persuasive. However, it is essential to avoid using inflammatory or offensive language.

Anticipating Counterarguments

Lawyers should identify potential weaknesses in their arguments and anticipate counterarguments that opposing counsel may raise. By anticipating counterarguments, lawyers can prepare effective responses and address any concerns the judge or jury may have. When opposing counsel raises a counterargument, lawyers should be ready to address it directly and explain why it is not persuasive.

Using Evidence Effectively

Evidence must be relevant to the case and help prove or disprove a particular fact. It must also be credible and reliable, meaning it must be trustworthy and believable. Evidence should be presented in a clear and concise manner, with any supporting documents or exhibits properly identified and authenticated. It should be used strategically to support the client's case and undermine the opposing party's arguments. This may involve highlighting the most critical evidence and downplaying less relevant evidence.

By following these principles, lawyers can present persuasive arguments that are likely to convince the judge or jury of the client's case

Building Relationships

Client Communication

Effective communication with clients is essential for building trust, maintaining a positive attorney-client relationship, and meeting client needs. This involves maintaining regular contact with clients to keep them informed about the progress of their case and to address any concerns or questions they may have, explaining legal matters clearly and understandably, avoiding legal jargon, providing regular updates on the case and listening attentively to the client's concerns and needs, responding empathetically and supportively, and treating clients with respect and dignity, regardless of their background or circumstances.

Courtroom Etiquette

Adhering to courtroom etiquette is essential for maintaining a professional and respectful environment. This includes respecting the judge, the court staff, and opposing counsel, dressing professionally and appropriately for court appearances, maintaining a calm and respectful demeanour in the courtroom, avoiding outbursts or disrespectful behaviour and adhering to the court's rules, including laws regarding evidence, objections, and courtroom procedures.

Networking

Building relationships within the legal community can be beneficial for expanding professional opportunities, gaining referrals, and staying informed about legal developments. This involves participating in legal conferences, seminars, and other events to meet other lawyers and legal professionals. Joining professional organisations, such as the American Bar Association or the Indian Bar Council, can provide networking and professional development opportunities. Developing relationships with other lawyers, judges, and court staff can help obtain referrals, share information, seek advice, and use social media and other online platforms to connect with legal professionals and build your professional network.

By building solid relationships with clients, maintaining appropriate courtroom etiquette, and networking within the legal community, lawyers can enhance their reputation, expand their professional opportunities, and provide better service.

PART III: THE DON'TS OF ADVOCACY

Ethical Violations

Conflict Of Interest

A conflict of interest arises when a lawyer's personal or professional interests could interfere with their ability to represent the client effectively. This can occur in various situations, including a lawyer unable to represent two clients with opposing interests in the same matter. For example, a lawyer cannot represent the plaintiff and the defendant in a lawsuit. A lawyer cannot also have a financial interest in the outcome of a case. This includes situations where the lawyer has a personal stake in the outcome, such as if they are a shareholder in a company that is involved in the litigation. He can also not represent a client if there is a close family relationship between the lawyer and the opposing party. A lawyer cannot represent a client if they previously represented the opposing party in the same matter or a related matter. To avoid conflicts of interest, lawyers must carefully screen potential clients and disclose any possible conflicts to their clients. If a conflict of interest arises, the lawyer must take steps to withdraw from the representation or obtain the client's informed consent.

Misrepresentation

Lawyers must be truthful in dealing with clients, courts, and opposing counsel. This includes refraining from making false or misleading statements. Misrepresentation can occur in a variety of ways, including:

- Making false statements about the facts of a case.
- Making misleading statements about the law.
- Presenting false or misleading evidence in court.
- Misrepresenting the client's position or instructions.

Making false or misleading statements can have serious consequences, including disciplinary action, sanctions, and criminal charges.

Ex Parte Communications

Ex-parte communications occur between a lawyer and a judge or opposing party without the knowledge or consent of the other side. These communications are generally prohibited, as they can compromise the fairness of the proceedings. Exceptions to the ex parte communication rule may exist in certain limited circumstances, such as when the communication is necessary to protect the client's interests or to address an emergency. However, lawyers should be cautious about engaging in ex-parte communications and only do so when required. By avoiding conflicts of interest, refraining from making false or misleading statements, and avoiding ex parte communications, lawyers can maintain the highest ethical standards and protect the interests of their clients.

Poor Communication

Failing To Respond

Prompt and effective communication with clients and the court is essential for maintaining a positive attorney-client relationship and ensuring that the case proceeds smoothly. Failure to respond to client inquiries or court orders can have serious consequences, including clients becoming frustrated or dissatisfied if they feel their lawyer is not responsive to their needs. Failure to respond to court orders can lead to delays in the case and potentially result in sanctions or adverse rulings. Clients may lose trust in their lawyer if they feel that they are being ignored or neglected. To avoid these problems, lawyers should respond to client inquiries and court orders promptly and effectively. This may involve scheduling regular meetings with clients, providing regular updates on the case, and responding to emails and phone calls promptly.

Using Legal Jargon

Legal jargon is a specialised language that lawyers and other legal professionals use. While it can help communicate with other legal professionals, it can also be confusing and off-putting to clients and the court. Lawyers should avoid using legal jargon whenever possible, especially when communicating with clients or the court. Instead, they should use plain language that is easy to understand. If a legal term is necessary, it should be explained in simple terms. By avoiding legal jargon, lawyers can ensure that their clients and the court understand the legal issues involved in the case and can make informed decisions.

Failing to Listen

Active listening is an essential communication skill that involves paying attention to what others are saying, understanding their perspective, and responding appropriately. Failure to listen can lead to misunderstandings, miscommunications, and a breakdown in the attorney-client relationship. When communicating with clients, witnesses, or opposing counsel, lawyers should:

- **Maintain Eye Contact:** Eye contact shows the lawyer is engaged and attentive.
- **Avoid Interruptions:** Allowing the speaker to finish speaking without interrupting.
- **Asking Clarifying Questions:** Asking questions to ensure that the lawyer understands what the speaker is saying.
- **Paraphrasing:** Restating the speaker's words in the lawyer's words to show they understand their perspective.
- **Empathy:** Showing empathy and understanding for the speaker's feelings and experiences.

By actively listening to clients and others involved in the case, lawyers can build trust, gather necessary information, and avoid misunderstandings.

Inadequate Preparation Lack of Research

Insufficient legal research can have severe consequences for a case, including:

- **Weak Arguments:** Without a strong foundation of legal research, lawyers may be unable to present persuasive arguments supporting their client's case.
- **Missed Opportunities:** Lawyers may miss important legal arguments or evidence if they do not conduct thorough research.
- **Ethical Violations:** In some cases, inadequate research can lead to ethical violations, such as making false or misleading statements about the law.

To avoid these problems, lawyers should conduct thorough legal research before proceeding. This may involve using legal databases, law libraries, and other resources to identify relevant statutes, case law, and legal treatises.

Poor Organization

Practical organisation is essential for presenting a clear and persuasive case. Poor organisation can lead to confusion, disorientation, and a loss of credibility.

When preparing for a case, lawyers should:

- **Create a Case Timeline:** A timeline can help organise the case's facts and identify critical events.
- **Organize Evidence:** Evidence should be organised in a way that is easy to access and understand. This may involve creating a database or filing system.
- **Outline Arguments:** Lawyers should outline their arguments clearly and logically. This will help ensure

that the presentation is well-structured and persuasive.

By organising their case effectively, lawyers can present their arguments clearly and compellingly.

Overconfidence

Overconfidence can be a dangerous trap for lawyers. Overestimating one's abilities can lead to complacency and inadequate preparation.

To avoid overconfidence, lawyers should:

- **Be Humble:** Recognize that even the most experienced lawyers can make mistakes.
- **Seek Feedback:** Ask colleagues and mentors for feedback on their work.
- **Continuously Learn:** Stay up-to-date on legal developments and best practices.

By remaining humble and seeking feedback, lawyers can avoid the pitfalls of overconfidence and ensure that they are providing the best possible representation for their clients. Inadequate preparation can have severe consequences for a case, including a weaker argument, missed opportunities, and ethical violations. By conducting thorough research, organising their case effectively, and avoiding overconfidence, lawyers can ensure they are adequately prepared to represent their clients.

CONCLUSION

Effective advocacy requires a delicate balance of legal knowledge, communication skills, and ethical conduct. By understanding and applying the principles outlined in this research paper, lawyers can enhance their effectiveness, protect their clients' interests, and maintain the highest standards of professional conduct. A deep understanding of relevant legal principles, statutes, and case law is essential for effective advocacy. Conducting thorough legal research is crucial for identifying relevant legal authorities and developing persuasive arguments. Effective communication is vital to building relationships with clients, presenting arguments persuasively, and understanding the perspectives of others involved. Adhering to ethical principles is essential to maintaining public trust in the legal profession and ensuring that lawyers act in the best interests of their clients. This includes avoiding conflicts of interest, refraining from making false or misleading statements and maintaining client confidentiality. Adequate preparation and organisation are essential for presenting a solid and persuasive case. This includes identifying key issues, gathering and organising evidence, and developing a clear and well-structured presentation. Building solid relationships with clients, opposing counsel, and the court is essential for effective advocacy. This involves maintaining open and effective communication, adhering to courtroom etiquette, and networking within the legal community. Lawyers should strive to continuously improve their legal knowledge and skills through continuing education and professional development. Lawyers should regularly reflect on their ethical obligations and strive to maintain the highest standards of professional conduct. Lawyers should seek feedback from colleagues and mentors to identify areas for improvement and enhance their advocacy skills. Building solid relationships with clients is essential for effective advocacy and client satisfaction. Lawyers should stay up-to-date on legal developments and changes to ensure they provide the best possible representation for their clients. Lawyers can enhance their advocacy skills, protect their client's interests, and contribute to

the advancement of the legal profession.

CHAPTER TWO

MASTERING PRESENTATION AND PUBLIC SPEAKING FOR LAWYERS

- Abdul Majid Khan

Abstract

Effective presentation and public speaking skills are critical competencies for legal professionals, shaping their ability to advocate persuasively and communicate complex legal arguments across various platforms—from courtrooms to client meetings. This guide explores the foundational techniques required to excel in public speaking, emphasising the importance of audience analysis, structured content, and confident delivery. Beginning with strategies for understanding diverse audiences, such as judges, juries, and clients, the guide highlights how tailored messaging fosters a more significant impact. It then addresses common public speaking challenges, offering practical solutions for overcoming anxiety and building a commanding presence.

A key focus is placed on structuring presentations for maximum clarity and engagement. By providing techniques to simplify intricate legal concepts and employ visual aids effectively, the guide helps lawyers ensure their arguments are both accessible and compelling. Furthermore, it delves into delivery techniques—such as vocal variety, body language, and interactive methods—that enhance a lawyer's presence and connection with the audience.

Additionally, ethical considerations unique to legal persuasion and the distinctions between courtroom presentations and other legal environments are examined. Through case studies and practical exercises, the guide provides real-world examples to solidify learning. Ultimately, this resource is designed to support lawyers in refining their public speaking skills, thus bolstering their advocacy and communication effectiveness in an increasingly competitive field.

Overview

Effective presentation and public speaking skills are vital for lawyers, as these abilities directly impact their capacity to advocate for clients, influence juries, and engage with various stakeholders. This overview outlines critical components essential for mastering these skills within the legal profession.

1. Understanding the Audience

- **Audience Analysis**: Identify your audience—judges, jurors, clients, or peers—and understand their needs and expectations.
- **Tailoring Your Message**: Adjusting your language, tone, and content to resonate with different groups, ensuring clarity and engagement.

2. Structuring Effective Presentations

- **Clear Framework**: Organizing content logically with a compelling introduction, well-structured body, and firm conclusion.
- **Engagement Strategies**: Using storytelling and real-life examples to make complex legal issues relatable and memorable.

3. Content Development

- **Simplicity and Clarity**: Breaking down complex legal jargon into straightforward language without losing the essence of the argument.
- **Evidence and Support**: Integrating case studies, statistics, and legal precedents bolsters your argument and credibility.

4. *Delivery Techniques*

- **Vocal Variety**: Using pitch, pace, and volume to maintain interest and emphasise key points.
- **Body Language**: Employ gestures, eye contact, and posture to convey confidence and effectively engage the audience.

5. *Visual Aids and Technology*

- **Effective Use of Visuals**: Designing clear, professional slides and incorporating other multimedia elements to enhance understanding and retention.
- **Technology Proficiency**: Familiarity with presentation tools and platforms to ensure smooth delivery.

6. *Audience Engagement*

- **Interactive Techniques**: Encouraging questions, discussions, and feedback to create a more dynamic and participatory environment.
- **Handling Objections**: Developing skills to manage dissenting views and counterarguments gracefully and effectively.

7. *Practice and Refinement*

- **Rehearsal Importance**: Engaging in regular practice to build confidence and smooth out delivery.
- **Feedback Mechanisms**: Seeking constructive criticism from peers and mentors to identify areas for improvement.

PART 1: Understanding Your Audience in Legal Presentations

Understanding your audience is fundamental to effective presentation and public speaking for lawyers. By identifying your audience, tailoring your message, and managing different stakeholder expectations, you can significantly enhance the impact of your communication. Here's how each component plays a critical role:

1. Identifying Your Audience

- **Who Are They?**: Recognizing the group you are addressing—a judge, jury, client, opposing counsel, or colleagues—is crucial. Each audience has different levels of familiarity with legal concepts and varying expectations.
- **Demographics and Background**: Consider age, professional background, cultural context, and legal knowledge. For example, a jury may need more background on legal terms compared to a room full of seasoned attorneys.
- **Psychographics**: Understand your audience's values, beliefs, and attitudes. A jury might respond better to emotional appeals, while a panel of judges might prefer

logical, well-structured arguments grounded in law.

2. Tailoring Your Message

- **Language and Tone**: Adapt your language to match the audience's level of understanding. Avoid legal jargon when speaking to clients or laypersons while using precise terminology in discussions with other legal professionals.
- **Content Relevance**: Focus on the aspects of your argument or presentation that matter most to your audience. For a client, emphasise how a legal decision impacts their specific situation. For a jury, illustrate how the evidence relates to the case.
- **Engagement Strategies**: Use stories, examples, and analogies that resonate with your audience. Relating legal principles to real-life situations can make your message more relatable and memorable.

3. Managing Different Stakeholder Expectations

- **Recognizing Diverse Interests**: Each stakeholder will have different interests and priorities. For example, clients may seek reassurance and clarity, while judges expect professionalism and adherence to legal standards.
- **Setting Clear Objectives**: Define your goal with your presentation for each audience segment. This could

include persuading a jury, informing a client, or seeking cooperation from opposing counsel.

- **Adapting Your Approach**: Be prepared to adjust your presentation style on the fly based on audience reactions. If a jury appears confused, be ready to clarify points. If clients express concern, address their worries directly to maintain trust.

PART 2: Fundamentals of Public Speaking in Legal Contexts

Mastering public speaking is essential for lawyers, as effective communication can significantly influence legal outcomes. Understanding the critical elements of an excellent presentation, overcoming fear and anxiety, and developing a confident presence are foundational to this skill set.

1. Key Elements of a Great Presentation

- **Clarity and Structure**: A well-organized presentation is critical. Lawyers should start with a clear outline with an engaging introduction, a logically flowing body, and a firm conclusion. Each section should support the overall argument or message.
- **Engaging Content**: Illustrate key points using compelling stories, analogies, and real-world examples. This approach not only makes the material more relatable but also helps to maintain audience interest. For instance, a lawyer might share a case study highlighting a legal principle's real-world implications.

- **Visual Aids**: Slides, charts, or other visuals can enhance understanding and retention. Lawyers should ensure that any visual aids are precise, professional, and directly relevant to the presented content.
- **Call to Action**: End with a solid call to action that reinforces the key takeaway. Whether persuading a jury or advising a client, a clear, actionable conclusion leaves a lasting impression.

2. Overcoming Fear and Anxiety

- **Preparation and Practice**: Thorough preparation is the most effective way to combat fear. Familiarity with the material builds confidence. Lawyers should rehearse their presentations multiple times, ideally in front of peers who can provide constructive feedback.
- **Mindfulness Techniques**: Practicing mindfulness or breathing exercises before a presentation can help manage anxiety. Techniques such as visualisation—imagining a successful presentation—can also reduce nervousness.
- **Focus on the Message**: Shifting attention from self-consciousness to the importance of the message can alleviate anxiety. Lawyers should remind themselves that the audience is interested in the content, not just the speaker.

3. Developing a Confident Presence

- **Body Language**: Confident body language is critical to effective public speaking. Lawyers should maintain eye contact, use appropriate gestures, and avoid closed-off postures. This body language communicates authority and engagement.
- **Vocal Control**: Developing a strong, clear voice is crucial. Lawyers should practice varying their tone, pace, and volume to emphasise essential points and maintain interest. A confident vocal delivery enhances credibility.
- **Authenticity**: Being genuine and authentic helps build trust with the audience. Lawyers should embrace their unique style and personality, as this authenticity fosters a connection with listeners.

Structuring Your Presentation in Legal Contexts

Effective presentation structuring is critical for lawyers. It enhances clarity and ensures that the audience grasps the essential points. Here's how to craft an engaging opening, develop a clear and logical flow, and use effective summaries and conclusions in legal presentations.

1. Crafting an Engaging Opening

- **Hook the Audience**: The opening should immediately grab the audience's attention. This could be through a compelling story, a provocative question, or a surprising fact about the legal issue. For instance, starting with a powerful case example can draw listeners in and highlight the topic's relevance.

- **Establish Credibility**: Briefly introduce your qualifications and experience related to the subject matter. This helps to build trust with the audience, especially in legal contexts where expertise is paramount.
- **State the Purpose and Agenda**: Clearly outline what you will cover in your presentation. This sets expectations and helps the audience follow along. For example, "Today, we will discuss the implications of recent changes in copyright law and how they affect your business."

2. Developing a Clear and Logical Flow

- **Logical Structure**: Organize your presentation to flow logically from one point to the next. Use a framework such as problem-solution or chronological order to guide the audience through the material. For instance, presenting a legal case chronologically—from the background to key developments and then to the outcome—can make complex information more digestible.
- **Use Transitions**: Clear transitions between sections help maintain momentum and guide the audience through your argument. Phrases like "Moving on to the next point" or "Now that we've established X, let's discuss Y" can keep listeners engaged.
- **Chunk Information**: Break down complex legal concepts into manageable segments. This might involve defining key terms before diving deeper into a legal

argument, ensuring that all audience members can follow along regardless of their legal background.

3. Effective Use of Summaries and Conclusions

- **Regular Summaries**: After discussing major points, briefly summarise what has been covered. This reinforces understanding and retention. For instance, after detailing a legal process, you might say, "To recap, we've examined the three critical steps in filing a motion."
- **Strong Conclusion**: The conclusion should tie everything together and reiterate the main points. It's essential to leave the audience with a clear understanding of the key takeaways. For example, "Understanding these legal changes is crucial for protecting intellectual property."
- **Call to Action**: End with a call to action, encouraging the audience to apply what they've learned. This could involve suggesting they consult a lawyer about their circumstances or consider how the discussed legal principles impact their decisions.

Content Development in Legal Presentations

Content development is crucial to mastering presentation and public speaking for lawyers. It involves researching and organising legal information, simplifying complex concepts, and effectively incorporating stories and case studies. Here's how each element contributes to impactful legal communication.

1. Researching and Organizing Legal Information

- **Thorough Research**: Lawyers must ensure their presentations are backed by accurate and up-to-date legal information, including statutes, regulations, case law, and relevant legal theories. Comprehensive research builds credibility and effectively informs the audience.
- **Organizing Information Logically**: Once the information is gathered, it should be organised in a way that makes sense to the audience. This might involve categorising information into themes or legal issues, creating an outline highlighting key points, and ensuring that each section flows logically.
- **Citing Sources**: Properly citing legal sources during the presentation enhances credibility and allows the audience to refer to the material later. Precise citations also demonstrate a commitment to ethical practice in legal communication.

2. Simplifying Complex Legal Concepts

- **Breaking Down Jargon**: Legal terminology can be dense and confusing for non-lawyers. Lawyers should strive to explain complex concepts in plain language, using analogies or everyday examples to clarify meaning. For instance, defining a contract using a relatable scenario can help demystify its components.

- **Using Visuals**: Visual aids like charts and diagrams can help simplify complex information. For example, a flowchart illustrating a legal process can help the audience grasp the steps involved.
- **Highlighting Key Takeaways**: Focusing on essential points and summarising them strategically during the presentation can reinforce understanding. Lawyers should emphasise the implications of these concepts for the audience, ensuring they recognise why the information is relevant.

3. Incorporating Stories and Case Studies

- **Storytelling Techniques**: Stories can be powerful tools in legal presentations, as they evoke emotion and make the material relatable. A lawyer might share a narrative about a past case to illustrate a legal principle or highlight a legal decision's human impact.
- **Real-World Case Studies**: Incorporating relevant case studies provides concrete examples and demonstrates how legal theories apply in practice. Discussing the outcomes of specific cases can clarify complex legal ideas and engage the audience's interest.
- **Personal Experiences**: When appropriate, sharing personal experiences can help build rapport with the audience. It can also remind us that behind every legal principle is a natural person affected by the law.

Visual Aids and Technology in Legal Presentations

Effective use of visual aids and technology can significantly enhance lawyers' communication skills in mastering presentation and public speaking skills. Here's how to design effective slides, use visuals to improve understanding, and implement best practices for technology in presentations.

1. Designing Effective Slides

- **Simplicity and Clarity**: Slides should be visually appealing but not cluttered. Use clear fonts, a consistent colour scheme, and minimal text to convey key points. A good rule of thumb is to limit the amount of text on each slide—aim for bullet points rather than long paragraphs.
- **Focus on Key Messages**: Each slide should convey one main idea or theme. This helps the audience absorb information without feeling overwhelmed. Use headings to delineate topics and reinforce the overall structure of the presentation.
- **Incorporating Visuals**: Use relevant images, graphs, or charts to illustrate key points. Visuals can aid comprehension, especially when explaining complex legal concepts or statistical data. Ensure that all visuals are high-quality and directly support the message.

2. Using Visuals to Enhance Understanding

- **Illustrating Concepts:** Visual aids like diagrams or flowcharts can simplify complex legal processes. For instance, a flowchart showing the steps of a litigation process can help clarify the sequence of events for the audience.
- **Creating Emotional Connections:** Images and stories can evoke emotions and make the content more relatable. For example, sharing a poignant image related to a case can humanise legal concepts and help the audience connect personally.
- **Highlighting Key Data:** Charts and graphs can effectively present data, making trends or comparisons easy to understand. Use these tools to illustrate statistics related to case outcomes, compliance rates, or other relevant metrics, ensuring that the data is visually accessible.

3. Best Practices for Using Technology in Presentations

- **Familiarity with Tools:** Lawyers should be proficient in the presentation software they plan to use (e.g., PowerPoint, Keynote). Familiarity with the tools can prevent technical difficulties and allow smoother presentation transitions.
- **Backup Plans:** Always have a backup of your presentation on a USB drive or cloud storage, and consider having printed handouts of key slides or information in case of technical issues. This preparedness helps maintain professionalism and ensures you can continue delivering your message

without interruption.

- **Engaging the Audience**: Incorporate interactive elements like polls or Q&A sessions to encourage audience participation. Technology can facilitate these interactions, making the presentation more dynamic and engaging.
- **Rehearsing with Technology**: Practice using your visual aids and technology in advance. This includes ensuring that all links work, videos play correctly, and that you can seamlessly transition between slides. Familiarity with your materials enhances confidence and delivery.

Delivery Techniques in Legal Presentations

Mastering delivery techniques is essential for lawyers seeking to communicate effectively in presentations. This involves mastering verbal and non-verbal communication, utilising vocal variety and emphasis, and employing body language and gestures. Here's how each element plays a crucial role in effective legal communication.

1. Verbal and Non-Verbal Communication

- **Verbal Communication**: This encompasses your spoken words' clarity, tone, and articulation. Lawyers should communicate clearly and at an appropriate pace, ensuring that their audience can easily follow along. Avoiding overly complex jargon when addressing non-legal audiences is essential to maintaining engagement and understanding.

- **Non-Verbal Communication**: Non-verbal cues such as facial expressions, eye contact, and posture play a significant role in receiving messages. Maintaining eye contact helps establish rapport and shows confidence, while open and relaxed body posture can make the speaker appear more approachable.
- **Alignment of Messages**: Ensuring that verbal and non-verbal messages are aligned enhances credibility. For instance, if a lawyer is discussing a serious topic, their tone and facial expressions should match the gravity of the message. Inconsistencies can create confusion and undermine authority.

2. *Vocal Variety and Emphasis*

- **Vocal Variety**: Pitch, volume, and pace changes can help maintain audience interest. A monotonous delivery can lead to disengagement while varying your vocal delivery can emphasise key points and enhance overall engagement.
- **Emphasis on Key Points**: Stressing important words or phrases through changes in volume or tone can highlight essential information. For example, raising your voice slightly can draw attention to the takeaway message when concluding a critical argument.
- **Pacing for Impact**: Pausing strategically can allow the audience time to absorb information and create suspense. For instance, pausing before revealing crucial evidence can enhance its impact.

3. Body Language and Gestures

- **Purposeful Gestures:** Hand gestures can help illustrate points and convey enthusiasm. However, gestures should be purposeful and not excessive, as overusing them can be distracting. For example, using a hand gesture to indicate size or direction can clarify complex information.
- **Movement:** Controlled movement can enhance engagement. Moving towards the audience during critical points can create a sense of connection, while stepping back can indicate a transition to a new topic.
- **Facial Expressions:** Conveying emotions through facial expressions can significantly enhance your message. A sincere smile when discussing positive outcomes or a concerned expression during serious discussions can deepen audience engagement.

Engaging Your Audience in Legal Presentations

Engaging the audience is critical to effective presentation and public speaking for lawyers. By utilising interaction techniques, handling questions and objections, and managing group dynamics, lawyers can enhance their presentations and foster a more collaborative environment. Here's how each aspect contributes to successful communication.

1. Techniques for Interaction

- **Encouraging Participation**: Actively inviting audience participation can make presentations more dynamic. Lawyers can use techniques like asking open-ended questions, conducting polls, or incorporating brief discussion breaks to stimulate engagement. For instance, prompting the audience to share their thoughts on a legal issue can foster a sense of involvement.
- **Utilizing Technology**: Tools such as audience response systems or apps can facilitate real-time interaction, allowing attendees to respond to questions anonymously. This approach can encourage more honest feedback and participation, especially in larger groups.
- **Creating a Collaborative Environment**: Establishing a comfortable atmosphere where the audience feels valued can enhance engagement. A lawyer can achieve this by acknowledging audience contributions, showing appreciation for questions, and being approachable throughout the presentation.

2. Handling Questions and Objections

- **Inviting Questions**: Setting aside specific times for questions can help manage audience inquiries without interrupting the flow of the presentation. For example, a lawyer might state, "I will take questions at the end of each section to ensure we stay on track."

- **Responding Effectively**: When faced with questions or objections, lawyers should listen carefully, acknowledge the concern, and respond thoughtfully. This demonstrates respect for the audience's perspective and helps build trust. Phrases like "That's a great question" can foster a positive dialogue.
- **Maintaining Composure**: It's essential to remain calm and composed, even when confronted with challenging questions. If unsure of an answer, it's acceptable to acknowledge that and offer to follow up later. This approach maintains credibility and shows professionalism.

3. Managing Group Dynamics

- **Reading the Room**: Lawyers should be attuned to the audience's reactions and adjust their delivery accordingly. Recognising when the audience seems disengaged or confused can prompt a shift in tone or the introduction of interactive elements to recapture their attention.
- **Addressing Diverse Perspectives**: In legal settings, audience members may have varying expertise and opinions. Lawyers should strive to acknowledge and address these differences in their presentations, ensuring all audience members feel included and respected.
- **Facilitating Discussions**: Encouraging small group discussions or breakout sessions can allow for deeper engagement and collaboration. This approach enhances understanding and fosters a sense of community among

attendees.

Conclusion

Mastering presentation and public speaking is an essential competency for lawyers, directly influencing their ability to advocate for clients, engage with various stakeholders, and communicate complex legal concepts effectively. In today's fast-paced and competitive legal environment, the ability to convey ideas persuasively is not merely advantageous; it is critical for success.

The Importance of Audience Understanding

Understanding the audience is the foundation of effective communication. Lawyers must recognize who they are speaking to—whether it's a jury, a judge, clients, or colleagues—and tailor their message accordingly. This involves not only adapting language and content but also employing techniques that resonate with the audience's values and expectations. By engaging in active audience analysis and customizing presentations, lawyers can foster a connection that enhances comprehension and retention.

Structuring Content Effectively

The structure of a presentation plays a pivotal role in clarity and impact. A well-organized presentation guides the audience through a logical progression of ideas, helping them to follow complex arguments without confusion. By crafting engaging openings, developing a coherent flow of information, and concluding with powerful summaries, lawyers can ensure that their key messages are understood and remembered.

Mastering Delivery Techniques

Delivery techniques are equally important in captivating and maintaining audience attention. Lawyers must hone their verbal and non-verbal communication skills, including vocal variety, emphasis, and body language. A confident presence, supported by purposeful gestures and effective eye contact, can enhance credibility and engagement. Moreover, employing vocal variety to emphasize critical points can significantly affect how the message is received.

Engaging the Audience

Audience engagement is crucial for a successful presentation. By utilizing interactive techniques, such as inviting questions and fostering discussions, lawyers can create a more dynamic environment. Handling questions and objections with poise not only reinforces the speaker's authority but also shows respect for the audience's perspectives. Managing group dynamics—recognizing varied expertise levels and facilitating inclusive dialogue—further enriches the presentation experience.

Utilizing Visual Aids and Technology

The strategic use of visual aids and technology enhances understanding and retention. Well-designed slides, relevant visuals, and effective use of presentation tools can significantly impact the audience's experience. By keeping visuals clear and aligned with the spoken content, lawyers can reinforce their arguments and make complex information more accessible.

Continuous Improvement

Mastering presentation and public speaking is an ongoing process. Lawyers should seek feedback, engage in regular practice, and remain open to new techniques and technologies. Participating in workshops or public speaking courses can also facilitate growth in these skills. By committing to continuous improvement, lawyers can adapt to changing audience needs and technological advancements.

Final Thoughts

In conclusion, mastering presentation and public speaking is vital for lawyers aiming to excel in their profession. Effective communication not only enhances advocacy in the courtroom but also strengthens client relationships and professional reputations. As lawyers refine their skills in audience engagement, content structuring, delivery techniques, and the use of technology, they will become more persuasive and impactful communicators. Ultimately, these skills lead to better legal outcomes, foster trust in the legal profession, and contribute to the overall effectiveness of the legal system. By embracing the art of public speaking, lawyers can enhance their ability to serve clients, influence outcomes, and make meaningful contributions to the legal discourse.

CHAPTER THREE

MOTIVATION IN LEGAL PRACTICE: KEY DRIVERS OF LAWYER PERFORMANCE

- Aditya Singh

Introduction

The legal profession is renowned for its demanding workload, high pressure, and long hours. Many lawyers remain deeply engaged and committed to their careers despite these challenges. This raises the question: what drives them? Understanding motivation in legal practice is vital for organisations seeking to cultivate a motivated and satisfied workforce.

This paper examines intrinsic motivators— personal fulfilment, professional autonomy, and intellectual engagement—and extrinsic motivators—such as financial compensation, professional recognition, and career progression. The research seeks to understand how these factors influence lawyers' performance and well-being and propose practical strategies for improving motivation within the legal sector.

Research Objectives:

- Identify critical intrinsic and extrinsic motivators for legal professionals.
- Analyse the impact of these factors on lawyer performance and job satisfaction.
- Investigate the challenges posed by the legal profession's demands on motivation.
- Offer strategies for enhancing motivation and well-being among lawyers.

Motivation Theories in Professional Contexts

Exploring the psychological theories of motivation that apply to professional settings is essential to understanding what drives lawyers.

Maslow's Hierarchy of Needs

Maslow's theory suggests that individuals are motivated by a hierarchy of needs, beginning with basic needs such as financial security and moving to higher needs like self-esteem and self-actualisation. Younger lawyers might focus on achieving economic stability in the legal profession, while more experienced lawyers seek recognition, autonomy, and mastery in their careers.

Self-Determination Theory (SDT)

SDT emphasises the importance of intrinsic motivation and highlights three core needs: autonomy, competence, and relatedness. Lawyers who feel empowered to make decisions, believe in their skills and have positive workplace relationships are more likely to experience intrinsic motivation, which fosters long-term job satisfaction.

Herzberg's Two-Factor Theory

Herzberg's theory separates motivators into hygiene factors (salary and job security) and true motivators (recognition and responsibility). In legal practice, while adequate compensation is crucial, genuine motivation stems from factors like the opportunity for professional growth and the ability to influence outcomes in meaningful cases.

MASLOW'S HIERARCHY OF NEEDS

Maslow's Hierarchy of Needs, developed by Abraham Maslow in 1943, is a psychological framework that categorises human needs into five levels, structured in a pyramid. According to this theory, individuals are driven to satisfy these needs in a particular order, from basic survival needs to higher, more complex aspirations. In the context of research work, this model can be applied to understand what motivates researchers and professionals to achieve higher levels of productivity and fulfilment.

The Five Levels of Maslow's Hierarchy of Needs

1. **Physiological Needs**: These are the most basic needs necessary for survival, such as food, water, shelter, and rest. In a research setting, this can relate to the need

for financial stability and a reliable income that allows individuals to cover essential living expenses. If these needs are unmet, researchers may struggle to focus on their work.

2. **Safety Needs**: Individuals seek security and stability after satisfying physiological needs. In research, this translates into job security, access to healthcare, and a safe working environment. Intellectual security—being able to conduct research without interference, fear of censorship, or undue stress—also falls under this category.
3. **Social Needs (Love and Belonging)**: Humans are naturally social, and once their safety is assured, they seek relationships and a sense of community. For researchers, this need is often fulfilled through collaboration, mentorship, and being part of a supportive academic or professional network. Interactions with peers, feeling valued in a research team, and belonging can significantly boost motivation.
4. **Esteem Needs**: Esteem needs include self-esteem and the desire for recognition from others. In a research context, this involves gaining respect from colleagues, recognition for one's work, and professional accomplishments like publishing research or presenting at conferences. External validation, such as awards and accolades, enhances self-esteem while developing expertise and confidence in one's research, fulfilling internal esteem needs.
5. **Self-Actualization**: The highest level in Maslow's hierarchy is self-actualisation, where individuals strive to realise their full potential. In the realm of research, this is reflected in the desire to innovate, solve complex problems, and engage with intellectually stimulating

challenges that align with personal interests and passions. At this stage, motivation comes from a deep sense of purpose and fulfilment in the work rather than external rewards.

Applying Maslow's Hierarchy in Research Work

Maslow's theory can help explain the varying motivation levels among researchers, depending on which unmet needs. For instance:

- If a researcher is struggling with job insecurity or insufficient pay, their focus may be more on meeting basic needs rather than pursuing innovative research.
- A lack of peer support or mentorship can lead to feelings of isolation, reducing motivation to engage fully in research activities.
- Offering recognition, career advancement opportunities, and professional development can meet esteem needs, encouraging researchers to produce higher-quality work.
- Once lower-level needs are fulfilled, researchers are more likely to reach self-actualisation, driving them to pursue groundbreaking research and realise their intellectual potential.

Self-Determination Theory (SDT)

Self-determination theory (SDT) is a psychological theory of human motivation developed by Edward Deci and

Richard Ryan in the 1980s. It focuses on the intrinsic and extrinsic factors that drive human behaviour, emphasising the importance of internal motivation in promoting well-being, productivity, and personal growth. The theory highlights three fundamental psychological needs for fostering intrinsic motivation and maintaining psychological health: autonomy, competence, and relatedness.

Critical Components of Self-Determination Theory

1. **Autonomy:**Autonomy refers to the need to feel in control of one's actions and decisions. In SDT, individuals are most motivated when they perceive they can make choices and direct their behaviour. Autonomy doesn't necessarily mean complete independence but rather having a sense of ownership and volition in what one does. For example, in a work or learning environment, when people feel they can approach tasks in their way or make decisions about their goals, they are more likely to be intrinsically motivated and engaged.
2. Competence refers to feeling adequate and capable in one's activities. People are more motivated when they believe they have the skills and knowledge to complete tasks and overcome challenges. SDT posits that individuals naturally seek growth, mastery, and development of their abilities. Environments that provide opportunities for skill development, constructive feedback, and appropriate challenges foster this sense of competence, leading to higher levels of

motivation and satisfaction.

3. Relatedness refers to the need to feel connected to others, belong, and have meaningful relationships. Humans are social creatures, and SDT emphasises that feeling supported, understood, and cared for by others enhances motivation. In both personal and professional settings, individuals are more likely to be engaged and motivated when they experience a sense of belonging and connection with colleagues, peers, or mentors.

Intrinsic vs. Extrinsic Motivation

SDT makes a critical distinction between intrinsic and extrinsic motivation:

- **Intrinsic Motivation:** Intrinsic motivation comes from within and involves doing something because it is inherently interesting, enjoyable, or fulfilling. When intrinsically motivated individuals engage in activities because they find them personally rewarding, not because of external pressure or rewards. For example, a researcher who explores a topic out of curiosity or a lawyer who takes on a case because of a deep sense of justice is motivated intrinsically. According to SDT, environments that satisfy autonomy, competence, and relatedness foster intrinsic motivation.
- **Extrinsic Motivation: Conversely, extrinsic motivation** involves doing something to achieve an external reward or avoid a punishment. It includes activities driven by outside factors, such as monetary incentives, grades, or social approval. While extrinsic motivation can drive behaviour in the short term, SDT argues that it is less

sustainable over time if some level of intrinsic satisfaction does not accompany it.

SDT suggests that people are more likely to feel fulfilled, be creative, and achieve long-term success when they are motivated intrinsically rather than relying solely on external rewards.

Different Forms of Extrinsic Motivation

Although extrinsic motivation is often associated with external rewards, SDT recognises that it can exist in various forms along a continuum, ranging from more controlled to more autonomous types of motivation:

1. External Regulation: Motivation driven entirely by external rewards or punishments. For example, working only for a paycheck or to avoid being reprimanded.
2. Introjected Regulation: Motivation that is somewhat internalised but still based on external pressures, such as guilt or the desire for approval from others. For example, we are working hard to avoid feelings of shame.
3. Identified Regulation: This occurs when individuals have internalised an external goal because they value it. For instance, lawyers work long hours because they believe in the importance of their work.
4. Integrated Regulation: The most autonomous form of extrinsic motivation, where external goals align with individual values and identity. This closely resembles intrinsic motivation, as people perform actions because they fully endorse them, even though external rewards may be involved.

SDT in Practice

Self-determination theory has been widely applied in various fields, including education, the workplace, healthcare, and sports, to foster motivation and improve performance. Key practices include:

- In Education: Teachers can foster intrinsic motivation by giving students more autonomy in approaching assignments, offering positive feedback to build competence, and creating a classroom environment where students feel supported and connected to others.
- In the Workplace: Managers can motivate employees by offering meaningful work that allows autonomy, opportunities for skill development, and fostering a sense of community within the team. For example, providing employees flexibility in achieving their goals can promote intrinsic motivation.
- In Healthcare: SDT has encouraged patient adherence to treatments and healthier behaviours by supporting autonomy in decision-making, helping patients feel competent to manage their health, and fostering positive relationships with healthcare providers.

Herzberg's Two-Factor Theory

Herzberg's Two-Factor Theory, also known as the Motivation-Hygiene Theory, was developed by psychologist Frederick Herzberg in the 1950s. This theory explains the factors that influence job satisfaction and motivation in the workplace. Herzberg found that job satisfaction and dissatisfaction arise from motivators and hygiene. Understanding this distinction is crucial for effectively enhancing employee motivation and ensuring job satisfaction.

Critical Concepts of Herzberg's Two-Factor Theory

Motivators (Intrinsic Factors): Motivators, also known as intrinsic factors, are those elements of a job that lead to satisfaction and motivate employees to perform better. These factors are related to the nature of the work itself and the personal growth it provides. They encourage employees to push beyond basic expectations and achieve higher performance levels. The presence of motivators leads to job satisfaction and motivation, while their absence may not cause dissatisfaction but will result in a lack of motivation or engagement.

Common Motivators:

- **Achievement:** The sense of accomplishment and personal success when tasks are completed effectively.
- **Recognition:** Being acknowledged and appreciated for good work.
- **Work Itself:** Finding job duties interesting, challenging, and fulfilling.
- **Responsibility:** Having autonomy and authority to make decisions in one's role.
- **Advancement:** Opportunities for career growth, promotion, and upward mobility.
- **Personal Growth:** The chance to learn new skills, face new challenges, and grow professionally.

Impact: When these motivators are present in the workplace, employees are more likely to experience job satisfaction and be intrinsically motivated, going beyond mere task completion to strive for excellence and innovation.

Hygiene Factors (Extrinsic Factors): Hygiene factors, also called extrinsic factors, do not lead to higher motivation or satisfaction when present, but their absence can cause dissatisfaction. These factors relate to the environment in which employees work rather than the work itself. Herzberg argued that addressing hygiene factors helps eliminate dissatisfaction but does not create motivation or job satisfaction. Essentially, hygiene factors "neutralise" dissatisfaction but do not promote engagement or fulfilment.

Common Hygiene Factors

- **Company Policies:** Fair and transparent organisational policies and procedures.
- **Supervision:** The quality of supervision and leadership that employees receive.
- **Working Conditions:** The physical work environment, including safety, comfort, and access to necessary resources.
- **Salary:** Adequate and competitive compensation and benefits.
- **Job Security:** Assurance that one's position is secure and employment is stable.
- **Work-Life Balance:** Adequate time off, flexible working hours, and respect for personal time.
- **Relationships with Colleagues:** The quality of interpersonal relationships with coworkers, supervisors, and subordinates.

Impact: The absence of these hygiene factors can lead to job dissatisfaction, demotivation, and even turnover. However, when hygiene factors are addressed and managed correctly, they create a neutral work environment rather than an actively motivating one.

Dual Nature of Job Satisfaction and Dissatisfaction

One of the core insights of Herzberg's theory is that job satisfaction and dissatisfaction are not on the same continuum. In other words, removing dissatisfaction (by improving hygiene factors) does not automatically create satisfaction, just as introducing motivators does not immediately erase dissatisfaction if hygiene factors are poor.

For example:

- Improving salary or working conditions (hygiene factors) may reduce complaints and dissatisfaction but will not necessarily inspire employees to perform at their best.
- On the other hand, increasing opportunities for advancement or recognising achievements (motivators) can significantly boost motivation and satisfaction, but only if hygiene factors are adequately addressed first.

Applications of Herzberg's Theory in the Workplace

1. **Job Design:** To enhance motivation, employers should focus on increasing motivators in the workplace. This can be done by enriching job roles with more responsibilities, opportunities for learning, and avenues

for career growth. Tasks that promote personal achievement and creativity should be included in job roles to boost engagement.

2. **Work Environment:** Hygiene factors such as a safe and pleasant physical work environment, fair compensation, and transparent company policies should be prioritised to reduce dissatisfaction. Organisations must ensure employees feel supported, respected, and valued in their work environment to prevent demotivation.
3. **Employee Recognition Programs:** Implementing systems of recognition for accomplishments or exemplary performance is essential to fulfilling the need for achievement and recognition, which are key motivators. Acknowledging employees' hard work helps reinforce positive behaviour and contributes to job satisfaction.
4. **Balancing Compensation and Growth:** While financial incentives (a hygiene factor) may not increase long-term motivation, they can reduce dissatisfaction. Pairing competitive compensation with opportunities for professional development and career progression (motivators) creates a balanced approach that can enhance overall motivation.
5. **Management and Leadership:** Effective supervision and leadership can address hygiene and motivator factors. Leaders should create an environment where employees feel supported (hygiene) while fostering autonomy, responsibility, and personal growth (motivators) to stimulate job satisfaction and long-term engagement.

Criticisms of Herzberg's Two-Factor Theory

While Herzberg's theory has been highly influential, it has faced some criticisms:

- **Individual Differences:** Some critics argue that the theory assumes all employees respond to motivators and hygiene factors similarly, overlooking individual differences in preferences, motivations, and expectations.
- **Methodological Issues:** Herzberg's original research relied heavily on interviews, which some researchers believe introduced bias. People are more likely to attribute positive experiences to themselves (internal motivators) and negative experiences to external factors (hygiene).
- **Over-Simplification:** Some have seen the clear separation of motivators and hygiene factors as too simplistic. Certain factors, such as salary, can be motivators and hygiene factors, depending on the context.

Intrinsic Motivation in Legal Practice

Intrinsic motivation comes from internal satisfaction and drives individuals to engage in activities for their inherent rewards. For lawyers, intrinsic motivation plays a significant role in career engagement and satisfaction.

Passion for Justice and Advocacy

Many lawyers are drawn to the profession because of a deep commitment to justice and the protection of legal rights. This drive is solid in public interest law, where lawyers feel they positively impact society. This sense of purpose can be a powerful motivator, even when facing challenges like extended hours or lower financial compensation.

Intellectual Challenge and Professional Mastery

The complexity of legal work often appeals to intellectually curious lawyers. The need to analyse intricate legal problems, apply critical thinking, and master new areas of law can serve as powerful motivators. The ongoing process of learning and improving their legal skills fosters a sense of accomplishment and professional fulfilment.

Autonomy and Decision-Making Power

Lawyers value autonomy in their work, whether independently or within a firm. The ability to make decisions and manage cases on their terms is a significant source of job satisfaction. Autonomy allows lawyers to feel in control of their professional lives, which enhances intrinsic motivation.

Social Impact and Fulfilment

In addition to intellectual challenges, many lawyers are motivated by the desire to make a difference in the lives of others. This is particularly true for lawyers in areas such as human rights law, civil rights law, and nonprofit legal services. The fulfilment that comes from positively impacting society can sustain motivation, even in adversity.

Extrinsic Motivation in Legal Practice

While intrinsic rewards are significant, extrinsic motivators from external sources also play a crucial role in driving lawyer motivation.

Financial Compensation

The legal profession, particularly in corporate law, is often associated with high salaries, bonuses, and financial rewards. Financial stability and the potential for high earnings are significant motivators for many lawyers. However, research indicates that beyond a certain threshold, increasing financial rewards has diminishing returns on long-term motivation.

Professional Status and Prestige

Lawyers often derive motivation from the social status and prestige associated with the profession. Achieving higher titles, such as partner or senior counsel, provides recognition and a sense of accomplishment. The respect afforded to successful lawyers within their firms and the broader legal community is an important motivator.

Job Security and Career Progression

The legal profession offers structured career paths, particularly in larger firms where progression from associate to partner is well-defined. Job security and the prospect of advancement are critical motivators for many lawyers. The potential for future financial rewards, greater autonomy, and leadership roles drives many lawyers to persist through challenging times early in their careers.

External Recognition and Validation

Being recognised for their work, whether through client feedback, industry awards, or accolades from peers, provides lawyers with a sense of validation. External recognition reinforces the sense of achievement and can be a strong motivator, particularly in competitive legal environments.

Impact of Organizational Culture on Lawyer Motivation

A law firm's culture plays a crucial role in shaping the motivation and engagement of its lawyers. Organisational culture, leadership, and support systems can either enhance or detract from motivation.

Leadership and Mentorship

Lawyers are more motivated when strong leaders provide mentorship and career development opportunities. Senior lawyers and firm partners who guide junior lawyers, provide constructive feedback, and invest in their professional growth can significantly boost motivation.

Collaborative vs. Competitive Work Environments

Workplace culture can vary significantly between law firms. Some firms emphasise collaboration and teamwork, fostering a supportive environment that enhances motivation. A hyper-competitive culture can demotivate lawyers by creating unnecessary tension and stress.

Professional Development Opportunities

Law firms prioritising training, mentorship, and skill development provide lawyers with new challenges and opportunities for growth. The prospect of advancing professionally keeps lawyers engaged and motivated to excel.

Strategies for Enhancing Lawyer Motivation

Law firms can implement several strategies to enhance lawyer motivation based on analysing motivational factors and challenges.

Work-Life Balance Initiatives

Law firms can adopt policies that promote a healthier work-life balance, such as flexible working hours, remote work options, and improved vacation policies. Firms that support the well-being of their lawyers are more likely to retain motivated and productive employees.

Recognition and Reward Programs

Law firms can implement systems that recognise and reward exceptional work. Regular performance-based bonuses, public recognition of accomplishments, and client feedback acknowledgement can help reinforce motivation.

Opportunities for Career Growth and Learning

Providing lawyers with career advancement opportunities and access to continuing education programs can help sustain motivation. Lawyers who feel challenged and see a path for growth are more likely to remain engaged in their work.

Mental Health and Wellness Support

Law firms can offer mental health resources such as counselling services, stress management workshops, and wellness programs to combat burnout and stress. Supporting lawyers' mental well-being is critical to sustaining motivation over the long term.

Conclusion

Motivation in the legal profession is driven by a combination of intrinsic and extrinsic factors that significantly impact job satisfaction and performance. Intrinsic motivators such as a passion for justice, intellectual engagement, and professional autonomy play a central role in keeping lawyers committed to their work despite the demands and pressures of the profession. On the other hand, extrinsic motivators like financial rewards, career progression, and external recognition also hold substantial influence, particularly in high-pressure areas like corporate law.

However, challenges such as burnout, poor work-life balance, and limited autonomy, especially for junior lawyers, can undermine motivation over time. To address these issues, law firms must foster an organisational culture that supports their lawyers' professional growth and personal well-being. Implementing flexible work policies, recognition programs, and mental health resources can improve motivation and long-term retention and engagement.

Ultimately, law firms that balance satisfying intrinsic and extrinsic motivational needs will cultivate a more productive, satisfied, and resilient workforce. By addressing the profession's rewards and challenges, lawyers can create an environment where lawyers perform well and find lasting fulfilment in their careers.

CHAPTER FOUR

THE ROLE OF COMMUNICATION IN ADVOCACY AND CLIENT RELATIONS

- *Divyansh Giri*

Abstract

Effective communication is pivotal in law, particularly in advocacy and client relations. This paper explores the multifaceted role of communication in legal advocacy and its impact on client relationships. It delves into various communication strategies, the importance of empathy, the role of non-verbal communication, and the effect of technology on lawyer-client interactions. By examining these aspects, the paper aims to highlight how proficient communication enhances legal practice, fosters client trust, and ultimately leads to more successful legal outcomes.

INTRODUCTION

In any relationship, communication is crucial, and this is also true for a lawyer's relationship with their clients. The success of a legal case can be greatly influenced by how well a client and their attorney communicate. As a result, it is essential that attorneys and clients have open channels of communication right once. In the legal field, communication is essential. Effective communication is essential for attorneys to fully comprehend their clients' legal issues. This entails being aware of the client's goals, the specifics of the case, and any significant due dates or restrictions. Better legal representation and advice can be given by a lawyer who pays attention to their client's requirements and worries.

However, clients and their solicitors also need to communicate well. It is crucial that they give their attorney all the facts they require about the case in question. Additionally, even if it could harm their case, clients must be honest about any pertinent information. The attorney can offer the finest possible legal defence thanks to this information.

COMMUNICATION IN ADVOCACY

A lawyer's persuasive communication skills can have a big impact on how a case turns out.

In the legal field, written communication is equally essential. Attorneys are required to create accurate and organised legal documents, including briefs, pleadings, and contracts. Confusion or ambiguity in these documents may have serious repercussions, including disagreements or even legal issues. Legal documents that are written clearly and succinctly are more likely to accurately communicate their intended message and safeguard the interests of their clients.

Furthermore, in negotiations, good communication is essential. On behalf of their clients, attorneys frequently participate in negotiations to arrive at advantageous settlements or agreements. Lawyers with strong communication skills are able to listen to the other side, discover common ground, and clearly communicate their clients' interests. Effective communication can help solicitors reach win-win agreements that might save the need for drawn-out legal proceedings.

Building trust with clients, persuading juries and judges, and communicating complex legal material are all made possible by effective communication, which is crucial in legal representation. The value of teaching communication skills at law schools to provide students the tools they need to be successful in the legal profession has come to light more and more in recent years. The purpose of this study is to examine how law schools' instruction in communication skills contributes to the development of persuasive strategies in legal advocacy. Effective communication is crucial to attaining favourable results in legal advocacy, according to numerous legal experts.

The act of arguing or pleading in support of a cause, concept, or policy is known as legal advocacy. It entails arguing on behalf of a client in front of a legislature, court, or other decision-making body. To effectively represent their clients, attorneys must communicate effectively. Since it allows solicitors to effectively communicate legal concepts, negotiate, and advocate for their clients, communication is an essential part of the legal profession in India. Nonetheless, a number of issues confront the Indian legal profession, one of which is the deficiency of proficient communication abilities among solicitors.

Persuasive Communication: Advocacy is inherently about persuasion. Lawyers must present their cases convincingly to judges, juries, and opposing counsel. Persuasive communication involves clear, concise, and compelling argumentation. Lawyers need to structure their arguments logically, use evidence effectively, and appeal to the emotions and values of their audience.

Legal Writing: Legal writing is another critical aspect of communication in advocacy. Well-crafted legal documents, including briefs, motions, and memoranda, are essential for presenting arguments in a clear and professional manner. Effective legal writing requires precision, clarity, and the ability to convey complex legal concepts in an understandable way.

Oral Advocacy: Oral advocacy skills are vital during trials, hearings, and negotiations. Lawyers must be adept at thinking on their feet, responding to questions, and adjusting their arguments based on the reactions of the judge or jury. Effective oral advocacy combines legal knowledge with rhetorical skill.

COMMUNICATION IN CLIENT RELATIONS

Lawyers can only devote so much time and effort. Working in the legal field frequently entails long hours and demanding responsibilities. The key to reducing stress for both you and your clients is to establish lines of communication that are realistic, sympathetic, and straightforward. Enhancing communication between attorneys and clients simplifies your work, promotes candid and open dialogue, fosters trust, and eventually results in victories.

Priority should be given to efficient communications between attorneys and clients. If you don't have it, you risk:

- Ignoring or undervaluing your client
- Important information is being forgotten by your client.
- Your relationships with your clients are deteriorating.
- Reduced opportunity to bargain with customers
- losing out on upcoming projects with that customer or company

Communication is necessary to establish clear channels of communication, and different conversations call for different channels. A meeting or phone call is necessary for an open discussion, although an email or text message could suffice for a brief update.

Establish when the preferred routes of communication are suitable and have an upfront discussion about them. Make sure your client is satisfied if you offer them updates via email on a frequent basis, and make sure your staff has the resources necessary to make the process go more smoothly. Think of software that enables automatic update sending. If your office is overloaded with calls, think about using contact centre AI solutions to route messages and enquiries to the appropriate person.

It's not always easy to be a good listener. It can seem like you've heard all a lawyer has to say because they deal with so many clients. And that is where the issue is. It can be tempting to switch off, assume things, or draw conclusions too quickly, but each individual, client, company, and situation is different. You're missing out on important information if you don't put your clients first.

The art of active listening involves more than merely hearing what is being said. It includes:

- Keeping eye contact, even during a video call!
- Observing nonverbal indicators, such as anxiety, fear, or anger, and using them to provide the right kind of assistance
- Posing open-ended enquiries to elicit additional details and demonstrate sincere interest
- To show that you are paying attentive attention, paraphrase the speaker's remarks and reflect them back.

One can have a deeper understanding of the client's feelings and thoughts by actively listening to them. By making one's client feel more at ease, one can gain their trust, encourage them to open up, and ultimately improve your service.

Even for experienced professionals, legal jargon might seem incomprehensible, so consider your clients' reactions when you're bombarding them with intricate legal jargon. Although jargon may facilitate communication between solicitors, clients may feel devalued, perplexed, and less confidence in your sincere intention to assist them after you have smiled and nodded throughout a consultation. When explaining legal concepts, use plain language. Make sure you thoroughly explain legal procedures to your customer in a way they can comprehend, and don't be scared to enquire if they have any questions.

Every client believes that their transaction or case is the most significant thing in the world. It is to them. However, their issue is only one of several significant obligations for you. Due of their hectic schedules, solicitors are unable to maintain continuous communication with every client. The secret to preventing future animosity is to set reasonable expectations early on. On the other hand, a client may be impatient or nervous. It's critical to have open and honest conversations about what is and is not feasible.

A crucial piece of information is missing from your case. The client is adamant that they told you this a few weeks ago over the phone. Even if you're certain they didn't, you're starting to question yourself. Another item that seems like common sense but is sometimes forgotten when there is a lot of information being exchanged is keeping thorough conversation logs. Keep track of emails and messages, record or take thorough notes during in-person conversations, and record phone and video calls when necessary. To help keep everything documented and safely saved, there are virtual assistant tools, cloud storage options, and CRM systems.

One of the simplest and most efficient ways to get better at something is to be open to criticism. After all, when asked, most people are delighted to provide comments. Getting positive feedback might make you feel more confident and keep doing what you're doing well. Even more valuable—and a little scary—is negative input. We may learn, develop, and strengthen our areas of weakness with the support of constructive criticism. Asking for feedback has two benefits: it gives you important insight into your own work and demonstrates to your clients that you care. Additionally, prospective clients searching for a reputable lawyer will be able to read your public request for feedback.

Building Trust: Trust is fundamental to the lawyer-client relationship. Open and honest communication helps build this trust. Lawyers must listen to their clients' concerns, explain legal processes clearly, and provide realistic expectations. Empathy and understanding are key components of effective client communication.

Managing Expectations: Managing client expectations is crucial for maintaining a positive relationship. Lawyers should communicate potential outcomes, risks, and the likely timeline of a case. Clear communication helps prevent misunderstandings and dissatisfaction.

Confidentiality: Maintaining confidentiality is a core ethical obligation for lawyers. Clear communication about confidentiality and its limits is essential for client trust. Clients need to feel secure that their information is protected.

NON-VERBAL COMMUNICATION

Body Language: Non-verbal communication, including body language, facial expressions, and eye contact, plays a significant role in interactions with clients and in the courtroom. Positive body language can reinforce verbal messages and convey confidence and competence.

Active Listening: Active listening is a crucial non-verbal communication skill. It involves fully concentrating on what the client is saying, acknowledging their concerns, and responding appropriately. This fosters a supportive environment and strengthens the lawyer-client relationship.

THE IMPACT OF TECHNOLOGY

The advent of technology has revolutionized communication in the legal profession, significantly impacting lawyer-client relations. One of the most notable changes is the introduction of digital communication tools, such as email, video conferencing, and client portals, which have streamlined and enhanced the way lawyers interact with their clients. These tools offer convenience and efficiency, enabling lawyers to provide timely updates, share documents, and conduct consultations without the need for in-person meetings. This is particularly beneficial for clients who may have mobility issues, live in remote areas, or have busy schedules that make frequent office visits impractical.

Email has become a primary mode of communication in the legal field, allowing for quick and efficient correspondence. Lawyers can easily share updates, answer questions, and provide documentation electronically, which speeds up the communication process. However, the reliance on email also comes with challenges. Lawyers must be vigilant about maintaining confidentiality and security, as email can be susceptible to hacking and other cyber threats. Using encrypted email services and secure file-sharing platforms can mitigate these risks and ensure that client information remains protected.

Video conferencing tools like Zoom and Microsoft Teams have also transformed client relations by providing a platform for face-to-face communication without the need for physical presence. This technology has been particularly valuable during the COVID-19 pandemic, when social distancing measures limited in-person interactions. Video conferencing allows lawyers to maintain a personal connection with their clients, which is essential for building trust and rapport. It also enables lawyers to observe non-verbal cues and body language, which can be crucial for understanding a client's emotional state and ensuring effective communication.

Client portals are another technological advancement that has improved lawyer-client communication. These portals provide a secure online space where clients can access case documents, track the progress of their case, and communicate with their lawyer. This level of transparency helps clients feel more involved and informed, reducing anxiety and uncertainty about their legal matters. Client portals also allow for better organization and management of case-related information, making it easier for lawyers to keep track of deadlines, appointments, and client communications.

Despite the many benefits of digital communication, there are potential drawbacks that lawyers must consider. The impersonal nature of electronic communication can sometimes hinder the development of a strong lawyer-client relationship. While emails and messages are efficient, they lack the warmth and personal touch of face-to-face interactions. Lawyers should strive to balance digital communication with regular phone calls or in-person meetings to maintain a personal connection with their clients.

Moreover, the use of social media has introduced new dynamics into lawyer-client communication. Social media platforms can be powerful tools for marketing and client engagement, allowing lawyers to share information, updates, and insights with a broader audience. However, they also pose ethical challenges and risks. Lawyers must navigate the fine line between professional and personal use of social media, ensuring that they maintain client confidentiality and avoid any appearance of impropriety.

Clear guidelines and policies on social media use can help lawyers manage these risks effectively.

Technology has also facilitated the rise of virtual law practices, where lawyers provide legal services exclusively online. This model offers flexibility and cost savings, both for lawyers and clients. Clients can access legal services from the comfort of their homes, and lawyers can reduce overhead costs associated with maintaining a physical office. However, virtual law practices require robust cybersecurity measures to protect client information and ensure compliance with legal and ethical standards.

Digital Communication: The rise of digital communication tools has transformed lawyer-client interactions. Email, video conferencing, and client portals provide convenient ways to communicate. However, lawyers must ensure that these methods do not compromise confidentiality and that they continue to build personal connections with clients.

Social Media:Social media offers new opportunities and challenges for legal communication. Lawyers can use social media to share information and engage with clients and the public. However, they must navigate ethical considerations and maintain professionalism online.

CONCLUSION

In the realm of legal practice, effective communication is fundamental to fostering robust lawyer-client relationships and achieving successful legal outcomes. The integration of technology into communication practices has brought about significant advancements, offering efficiency and transparency. Digital tools such as email, video conferencing, and client portals have revolutionized how lawyers interact with their clients, allowing for timely updates, seamless document sharing, and virtual consultations. These technologies not only enhance the client experience but also enable lawyers to maintain close and continuous contact, crucial for building trust and rapport.

However, the shift towards digital communication also poses challenges. The impersonal nature of electronic interactions can sometimes undermine the development of strong personal connections. To counter this, lawyers must balance the use of technology with traditional communication methods, such as phone calls and in-person meetings, to ensure clients feel valued and understood. Furthermore, the increased reliance on digital tools necessitates stringent measures to protect client confidentiality and data security. Implementing encrypted communication channels and secure client portals is essential to safeguarding sensitive information.

The rise of social media and virtual law practices further illustrates the transformative impact of technology on the legal profession. While these platforms offer new opportunities for client engagement and cost-effective service delivery, they also require careful management to navigate ethical considerations and maintain professional standards.

The role of communication in advocacy and client relations, thus, is ever-evolving, shaped by technological advancements that offer both opportunities and challenges. By embracing these innovations and addressing their associated risks, lawyers can enhance their communication practices, build stronger client relationships, and ultimately achieve better legal outcomes. Effective, empathetic, and secure communication remains the cornerstone of successful legal practice, ensuring clients feel supported and informed throughout their legal journey.

CHAPTER FIVE

PERSONALITY IN LAW: ITS IMPACT ON LEGAL COMMUNICATION

- Purab Chaudhary

Abstract

This paper investigates the intricate relationship between personality traits and legal communication, highlighting the significant influence these traits have on how legal professionals such as lawyers, judges, and negotiators interact within their professional environments. It delves into the psychological aspects of personality, examining how traits like extraversion, agreeableness, conscientiousness, and emotional stability shape advocacy strategies, courtroom management, negotiation tactics, and the attorney-client relationship. The study underscores personality's critical role in shaping communication styles, decision-making, and legal outcomes.

By focusing on personality-driven factors, this paper reveals how personal characteristics can enhance or hinder various facets of legal practice, influencing legal proceedings' efficiency, fairness, and effectiveness. It also explores how legal professionals can leverage an understanding of their own and others' personality traits to improve communication, foster trust with clients, and optimize courtroom performance, ultimately contributing to a more equitable and just legal system.

INTRODUCTION

Legal communication is a cornerstone of the justice system, functioning as the means through which laws are interpreted, argued, and enforced. This form of communication includes the structured exchange of information, evidence, arguments, and decisions among key legal stakeholders—lawyers, judges, juries, and clients. At first glance, success in the legal field may seem to depend primarily on one's command of legal knowledge, analytical skills, and technical expertise. However, an often overlooked yet crucial element in this process is the influence of personality traits on the effectiveness of legal communication.

Personality is a complex combination of thoughts, emotions, and behavioural patterns consistently manifest over time. It shapes how individuals respond to various situations and interact with others. In the legal context, the personality of a lawyer, judge, client, or juror can significantly affect how they engage with legal issues, present information, and influence case outcomes. Traits such as extraversion, conscientiousness, agreeableness, openness to experience, and emotional stability (commonly called the "Big Five" personality traits) directly affect a legal professional's ability to communicate persuasively, manage relationships, and negotiate effectively.

This paper explores the intersection of personality and legal communication, examining how personality traits affect vital areas of the legal process, such as advocacy, courtroom management, and negotiation. By understanding the role of personality in legal communication, legal professionals can optimise their interpersonal interactions, improve advocacy, and contribute to more effective and equitable legal outcomes.

The Big Five Personality Traits in Legal Communication

The "Big Five" personality traits—extraversion, agreeableness, conscientiousness, emotional stability, and openness to experience—offer a valuable framework for analysing the impact of personality on legal communication. These traits can influence how lawyers, judges, and other legal participants communicate, advocate, and make decisions in the legal setting.

1. Extraversion

Extraversion is characterised by sociability, assertiveness, and a tendency to seek stimulation in social interactions. In the legal field, extroverted individuals often excel in situations that require public speaking, client engagement, and negotiation. Lawyers high in extraversion are typically confident advocates comfortable presenting arguments in court, addressing juries, and cross-examining witnesses.

Their outgoing nature enables them to communicate persuasively and establish rapport with clients, judges, and colleagues.

Extraverted lawyers may exhibit a dynamic and engaging communication style in courtroom settings, which can captivate juries and create a favourable impression. Their ability to think on their feet and assert their position confidently allows them to handle pressure effectively during trials. This is particularly important in adversarial legal systems where oral advocacy is critical. However, extroverted individuals may sometimes overpower quieter voices, potentially overshadowing more reserved or cautious approaches to legal argumentation.

On the other hand, extraversion can also present challenges. For instance, highly extroverted lawyers may struggle in situations that require deep reflection, patience, and listening, such as client consultations or detailed case analyses. Their preference for action and social interaction may lead them to overlook the importance of thorough research and preparation, mainly when complex cases require meticulous attention to detail.

2. Agreeableness

Agreeableness is associated with empathy, cooperation, and a focus on maintaining harmony in relationships. In legal communication, lawyers with high agreeableness tend to be compassionate advocates who prioritise their client's needs and well-being. They are effective in mediation and negotiation contexts, where a cooperative and non-confrontational approach is often required to achieve mutually beneficial outcomes. Their ability to understand and accommodate the perspectives of opposing parties can facilitate smoother negotiations and conflict resolution.

In the courtroom, agreeable lawyers may be seen as approachable and sincere, qualities that can enhance their credibility and foster trust among jurors, judges, and clients. These lawyers are often skilled in presenting arguments that emphasise fairness and moral responsibility, appealing to the emotions and values of their audience.

However, excessive agreeableness may hinder a lawyer's ability to represent their client's interests in adversarial settings assertively. Lawyers who prioritise harmony and avoid conflict may struggle to engage in aggressive cross-examinations or challenge the opposing party's arguments effectively. This can be a disadvantage in high-stakes litigation, where assertiveness and strategic confrontation are necessary to protect a client's rights.

3. Conscientiousness

A strong sense of responsibility characterises Conscientiousness, attention to detail, and a focus on achieving goals through organised and disciplined behaviour. In legal communication, conscientious lawyers are known for their thoroughness and reliability. They are meticulous in their research, ensuring that legal documents, briefs, and contracts are accurate and well-crafted. Their communication style tends to be structured, logical, and precise, critical for drafting arguments, analysing case law, and preparing for litigation.

In courtroom advocacy, conscientious lawyers are likely to present well-organized and coherent arguments backed by solid evidence and clear reasoning. Their attention to detail allows them to anticipate potential challenges and address them proactively, strengthening their case and enhancing their credibility. Conscientiousness is closely linked to time management and the ability to meet deadlines, both essential in the fast-paced and demanding legal environment.

While conscientiousness is generally seen as a positive trait in the legal profession, it can also have drawbacks. Overly conscientious lawyers may become overly cautious, focusing so much on perfecting details that they struggle to make quick decisions or adapt to unexpected changes during trials or negotiations. Furthermore, their methodical nature may make them less flexible in situations that require creative problem-solving or improvisation.

4. Emotional Stability (or Neuroticism)

Emotional stability, the opposite of neuroticism, refers to an individual's ability to remain calm, composed, and resilient under pressure. In legal communication, emotional stability is crucial for maintaining professionalism in high-stress environments, such as during trials or intense negotiations. Lawyers with high emotional stability can manage their emotions effectively, which helps them stay focused and rational even in adversity. This trait is precious when emotional outbursts or anxiety could undermine the lawyer's credibility or weaken their arguments.

Judges also benefit from emotional stability. This allows them to remain impartial and make decisions based on facts and legal principles rather than being swayed by personal emotions or external pressures. A calm and objective judge creates a stable and fair courtroom environment, ensuring justice is served without emotional bias.

Conversely, lawyers and judges with low emotional stability may struggle to manage stress, leading to emotional reactions that can cloud their judgment and hinder effective communication. Lawyers prone to anxiety or frustration may struggle to articulate their arguments clearly or engage in productive negotiations. In extreme cases, emotional instability can lead to ethical lapses or unprofessional conduct, undermining the lawyer's effectiveness and damaging their reputation.

5. Openness to Experience

Openness to experience is associated with creativity, curiosity, and a willingness to explore new ideas and perspectives. In legal communication, lawyers who score high on openness are likely to approach legal problems with innovation and flexibility. They are open to considering unconventional legal arguments or novel interpretations of statutes, which can be particularly useful in cases involving complex or evolving law areas, such as intellectual property, technology law, or environmental law.

Open-minded lawyers are also more likely to adapt their communication style to suit different audiences, whether a jury, a judge, or a client. Their ability to think outside the box can lead to creative solutions during negotiations or dispute resolution processes, helping parties reach agreements that might not have been possible through traditional approaches.

However, there are potential drawbacks to high levels of openness in legal practice. Lawyers who are overly focused on exploring new ideas may become distracted or lose sight of practical solutions. Innovative arguments may sometimes be too risky or speculative, leading to unfavourable court outcomes. Furthermore, highly open lawyers may struggle to adhere to the formal and rigid structures that often characterise legal procedures.

The Impact of Personality on the Attorney-Client Relationship

The attorney-client relationship is a critical component of legal practice, as it forms the foundation for effective communication, trust, and representation. Personality traits significantly shape this relationship, influencing how lawyers interact with clients, gather information, and advocate.

Agreeable and emotionally stable lawyers tend to excel at building rapport with clients. Their empathetic nature allows them to understand their clients' needs and concerns, fostering trust and open communication. Clients are more likely to feel heard and valued when working with an approachable and emotionally stable lawyer, which can lead to a more productive and collaborative relationship.

Conversely, highly extroverted lawyers may be more assertive in leading discussions and providing advice, which can be advantageous when clients need firm guidance. However, overly extroverted lawyers may dominate conversations, potentially alienating clients who prefer a more balanced or consultative approach.

Personality traits also influence how lawyers manage client expectations and deliver difficult news. Lawyers who are emotionally stable and conscientious are more likely to handle challenging conversations with professionalism and care, ensuring that clients are well-informed without being overwhelmed. On the other hand, lawyers with low emotional stability may struggle to manage their emotions during such discussions, which can lead to miscommunication or strained relationships.

Personality in Courtroom Dynamics

Courtroom dynamics are another area where personality plays a crucial role in shaping legal communication. The personalities of lawyers, judges, jurors, and witnesses can significantly affect the tone and flow of legal proceedings.

As the ultimate authority in the courtroom, judges set the tone for legal proceedings through their communication style, often influenced by their personality traits. A judge who is high in conscientiousness and emotional stability is likely to run a well-organized and impartial courtroom, ensuring that procedures are followed and that all parties are involved.

Personality and Legal Negotiation

Negotiation is a critical aspect of legal practice, often serving as a preferred method for resolving disputes without resorting to costly and time-consuming litigation. In a legal setting, negotiations occur in various forms, ranging from informal conversations between opposing parties to formalised mediation or arbitration processes. Personality traits play a significant role in how legal professionals approach and manage these negotiations, influencing the outcome and the parties' satisfaction.

Understanding how different personality traits, such as agreeableness and extraversion, influence negotiation tactics and outcomes is essential for legal practitioners aiming to enhance their negotiation skills. While agreeableness often leads to collaborative and solution-focused strategies, extraversion can bring assertiveness and persuasion into the negotiation. However, these traits also present distinct challenges that negotiators must know to avoid common pitfalls. This paper will expand on the influence of these two key traits—agreeableness and extraversion—in legal negotiations, exploring their strengths, weaknesses, and the broader impact on the negotiation process.

The Importance of Negotiation in Legal Practice

Negotiation is an essential skill in legal practice, utilised in nearly every area of law. Whether dealing with corporate mergers, employment disputes, or family law matters, legal professionals must frequently negotiate to reach agreements that benefit their clients.

Negotiations in legal practice can take many forms, including:

1. **Settlement Negotiations:** These are often employed to resolve civil disputes, such as personal injury claims, contract disputes, or business disagreements. Lawyers representing both sides typically aim to reach a financial or behavioural settlement that satisfies all parties without going to trial.

2. **Mediation:** A neutral third party (the mediator) helps the disputing parties reach a mutually agreeable resolution. Mediation is typical in family law, labour disputes, and commercial conflicts. The goal is to foster collaboration and create an agreement that both parties can accept.

3. **Arbitration:** Arbitration is a more formal process in which an arbitrator makes a binding decision on the dispute. While arbitration has elements of negotiation, it

also has judicial characteristics and may not allow for as much flexibility as other forms of negotiation.

4. Plea Bargaining: In criminal law, plea bargaining is a form of negotiation where the defence and prosecution negotiate terms to resolve a criminal case, often resulting in the defendant pleading guilty to a lesser charge in exchange for a more lenient sentence.

The Influence of Agreeableness in Legal Negotiation

Agreeableness, one of the "Big Five" personality traits, is characterised by empathy, cooperativeness, and a focus on maintaining positive social relationships. Lawyers high in agreeableness are often effective in fostering collaboration, building rapport with opposing parties, and seeking mutually beneficial outcomes. However, agreeableness can be both a strength and a potential weakness in legal negotiation, depending on the dispute's context and nature.

Strengths of High Agreeableness in Negotiation

1. Collaboration and Compromise: Lawyers who score high agreeableness are naturally inclined to prioritise cooperation and compromise. This trait is precious in mediation settings, where the goal is often to reach a consensus that satisfies both parties. An agreeable lawyer will strive to find common ground, listen attentively to the concerns of all involved, and work towards a solution that promotes harmony. This collaborative approach can de-escalate tensions and facilitate a faster, more amicable resolution to the dispute.

2. Empathy and Understanding: High levels of agreeableness are associated with empathy, which allows lawyers to understand the emotional needs and motivations of the opposing party. By being attuned to these underlying emotions, agreeable lawyers can craft negotiation strategies that address the dispute's legal or financial aspects and the personal concerns of the parties involved. This can help create more sustainable agreements that both parties are satisfied with, reducing the likelihood of future conflicts.

3. Building Trust: Agreeable lawyers often excel at building trust, a crucial component of successful negotiation. Their sincerity and cooperation can foster a more open and transparent dialogue, encouraging the other party to reciprocate with honesty and good faith. Trust is crucial in long-term negotiations, such as business partnerships or family law cases. When both sides trust that the lawyer is acting in the best interests of all parties, negotiations are more likely to progress smoothly.

Challenges of High Agreeableness in Negotiation

1. Risk of Over-Compromise: While compromise is a valuable negotiation skill, agreeable lawyers may sometimes prioritise cooperation to the detriment of their client's best interests. To maintain harmony, agreeable lawyers may concede too much or agree to less favourable terms to their clients than they should. This is particularly problematic in adversarial negotiations, where the opposing party may exploit the lawyer's willingness to compromise.

2. Difficulty in Adversarial Settings: Agreeable lawyers may struggle in negotiations that require a more confrontational or competitive approach. For example, in high-stakes corporate disputes or litigation, where the goal is to secure a win for one party, an overly cooperative stance can be perceived as a sign of weakness. Opposing counsel may exploit this by pushing for more aggressive terms, knowing that the agreeable lawyer is unlikely to return with equal force.

3. Balancing Advocacy with Cooperation: One of the biggest challenges for agreeable lawyers is balancing advocating for their clients and maintaining a cooperative approach. While seeking solutions that benefit all parties is essential, a lawyer's primary responsibility is acting in their client's best interests. Agreeable lawyers must be careful not to compromise on critical issues that could negatively impact their clients, even if it means creating some conflict during negotiations.

The Role of Extraversion in Legal Negotiation

Extraversion, another of the Big Five personality traits, is characterised by sociability, assertiveness, and a tendency to seek out stimulating environments. Lawyers who score high in extraversion are often confident and persuasive, qualities that can be highly effective in negotiation settings, particularly adversarial ones. However, like agreeableness, extraversion has strengths and weaknesses in legal negotiation.

Strengths of High Extraversion in Negotiation

1. Persuasive Communication: Extraverted lawyers are strong communicators who thrive in social interactions. In negotiations, their ability to articulate their client's position clearly and assertively can be a powerful tool for persuasion. Extraverts can often present arguments compellingly and confidently, influencing the opposing party to agree to favourable terms. Their charisma and ability to engage others can also help to keep the negotiation process dynamic and focused.

2. Comfort with Confrontation: Unlike agreeable lawyers, extroverted lawyers are generally more comfortable with confrontation and are not afraid to push back when necessary. This assertiveness can be an asset in adversarial negotiations, where standing firm on key issues is critical to achieving the best outcome for the client. Extraverts are less likely to shy away from making bold demands or challenging the opposing party's position, which can give them an advantage in high-stakes negotiations.

3. Confidence and Presence: In legal negotiations, confidence can be a critical factor in shaping the perceptions and behaviour of the opposing party. Extraverted lawyers often exude confidence, making them appear more credible and authoritative during negotiations. This commanding presence can influence the other party to take the lawyer's arguments more seriously. It may create a sense of pressure to reach an agreement on terms favourable to the extraverted lawyer's client.

4. Engagement and Energy: Extraverts tend to bring a high level of energy to negotiations, which can help to maintain momentum and prevent discussions from stagnating. Their enthusiasm for social interaction can keep both parties engaged, increasing the likelihood of resolving.

This ability to maintain focus and drive can be precious in long or complex negotiations.

Challenges of High Extraversion in Negotiation

1. Risk of Over-Assertiveness: While assertiveness can be an asset in negotiation, extroverted lawyers must be careful not to cross the line into aggression. Overly assertive or domineering behaviour can alienate the opposing party and create unnecessary conflict, making it more difficult to reach an agreement. In some cases, an extravert's assertiveness may be perceived as bullying, leading to a breakdown in communication and increasing the likelihood of litigation rather than settlement.

2. Lack of Listening: One potential downside of extraversion in negotiation is the tendency to dominate conversations. Extraverts may focus more on expressing their views and persuading others at the expense of actively listening to the other party's concerns and needs. This can result in missed opportunities for compromise or creative solutions, as the extraverted lawyer may not fully understand the other party's position.

Conclusion

Personality is a critical yet frequently underappreciated element in legal communication. The traits of legal professionals—whether they are lawyers, judges, or negotiators—profoundly influence their advocacy methods, interactions with clients, and effectiveness in the courtroom or during negotiations. Recognising how personality traits such as extraversion, agreeableness, conscientiousness, emotional stability, and openness to experience shape communication allows legal practitioners to refine their strategies and enhance their overall performance.

Professionals can better adapt their communication styles by integrating psychological insights into legal practice to suit various contexts and challenges. This awareness can foster more productive client relationships, improve courtroom dynamics, and contribute to more successful negotiations. Moreover, an understanding of personality can help legal professionals navigate the complexities of their roles with greater empathy and emotional intelligence, promoting fairness and integrity within the legal system.

In conclusion, by acknowledging and incorporating personality influence into legal communication, the legal profession can elevate the quality of legal discourse. This, in turn, can lead to more effective advocacy, greater client satisfaction, and, ultimately, more just outcomes in the legal process. As the legal field evolves, a deeper appreciation of personality's role will be essential for ensuring a more equitable and responsive justice system.

CHAPTER SIX

COMPONENTS OF CLIENT INTERVIEWS: LISTENING, QUESTIONING AND GATHERING INFORMATION

- *Abhishek Agarwal*

Abstract

Client interviews are a cornerstone of effective legal practice, serving as the primary mechanism for understanding client needs, gathering critical information, and establishing trust between lawyers and clients. This paper explores the essential components of client interviews—listening, questioning, and information gathering—within the context of Indian law. It highlights how active listening helps lawyers comprehend a client's case's facts and emotional undertones, fostering a stronger lawyer-client relationship. Strategic questioning techniques are examined for extracting relevant details and clarifying legal issues, while systematic information gathering is critical for ensuring accurate legal representation.

The research also addresses the ethical obligations lawyers must adhere to, including confidentiality and compliance with the principles outlined in the Advocates Act and the Indian Evidence Act. Case law illustrating the consequences of poor interviewing practices is analysed to reinforce the need for skilful interviewing. Additionally, the paper considers the challenges posed by cultural diversity, emotional barriers, and communication issues in client interviews, offering insights into how legal professionals can adapt their approach to meet these challenges.

By enhancing listening, questioning, and information-gathering skills, lawyers can improve client outcomes and satisfaction, ultimately contributing to the success of legal representation in India.

Introduction

Client interviews are significant in the Indian legal system as they are the foundational step in establishing a solid lawyer-client relationship. These interviews are not merely formalities but crucial for building trust, gaining insights into the client's needs and objectives, and gathering critical facts and information that form the basis of legal advice and representation. In many cases, the success of legal representation hinges on the thoroughness of the information gathered during the interview process, making this phase indispensable.

A well-conducted client interview can be a pivotal moment in understanding the client's legal issues, the context of their concerns, and any underlying factors that may affect the case. It also helps the lawyer manage client expectations and set the groundwork for a clear strategy. This is especially important in the Indian legal system, where cultural, social, and linguistic nuances may also influence the approach to legal advice and proceedings.

The effectiveness of a client interview depends mainly on the skill set of the interviewer—the lawyer. Active listening, empathetic communication, and the ability to ask pertinent and probing questions are essential qualities that allow a lawyer to uncover the necessary details without overwhelming or alienating the client. This also includes the lawyer's ability to create a safe and comfortable environment where the client feels free to disclose all relevant information, even those facts that may be sensitive or potentially damaging to their case.

Another critical aspect of the client interview process is the systematic organisation and documentation of the information obtained. A lawyer must gather and categorise information to ensure it can be used effectively for case analysis and strategy development. Failure to do so can lead to inaccurate facts, overlooked details, and a weaker legal argument.

Furthermore, lawyers must conduct these interviews while adhering strictly to the ethical and professional standards that govern their practice. This includes maintaining client confidentiality, providing competent and diligent representation, and avoiding conflicts of interest. Governing bodies, such as the Bar Council of

India, impose these standards to ensure that legal practitioners act in their client's best interests while upholding the legal profession's integrity.

Listening

Importance of Listening in Legal Context

Effective listening is vital for lawyers to comprehend the nuances of a client's case, assess their emotional state, and build a trustworthy relationship. Miscommunication can lead to flawed legal strategies or ethical issues.

Legal practitioners often encounter clients in distressing situations, such as criminal charges or family disputes. Active listening allows lawyers to understand the facts and emotional context of the client's problem. This understanding is essential for formulating strategies that resonate with the client's needs and expectations.

Types of Listening

- **Active Listening**: Engaging fully with the client, reflecting on their words, and providing feedback. Active listeners focus on the speaker without distractions, showing interest through verbal affirmations and body language.
- **Empathetic Listening**: Recognizing and validating the client's feelings and concerns. This type of listening goes beyond the content of what is said to acknowledge the emotional undertones. For example, saying, "It sounds like you're stressed about this situation," can

help clients feel heard and understood.

Techniques for Effective Listening

- **Nonverbal Communication**: Maintain eye contact and use open body language. Nonverbal cues are powerful in communication and often speak louder than words.
- **Creating a Conducive Environment**: Ensuring privacy and minimising distractions during the interview. A comfortable setting can encourage clients to speak freely. This includes choosing a quiet room, eliminating background noise, and ensuring confidentiality.
- **Feedback Mechanisms**: Summarizing and paraphrasing client statements to confirm understanding. Techniques such as reflective listening, where the lawyer restates what the client has said, can help clarify points and demonstrate that the lawyer is engaged.

Challenges in Listening

- **Cognitive Overload**: Lawyers often have to process large amounts of information quickly, affecting their ability to listen effectively.
- **Emotional Barriers**: Clients may be distressed or anxious, making it challenging to communicate clearly. Lawyers must navigate these emotional barriers to facilitate effective communication.

Questioning

Importance of Questioning

Strategic questioning helps lawyers clarify legal issues, uncover critical facts, and assess the validity of a client's claims. This process is essential for formulating effective legal strategies. Questions guide the conversation, directing it toward pertinent issues while allowing the lawyer to gain deeper insights into the client's situation.

Types of Questions

- **Open-Ended Questions**: Elicit detailed responses (e.g., "What events led to your legal issue?"). These questions encourage clients to elaborate and provide more context.
- **Closed-ended questions: These questions help confirm facts. They can be used to obtain specific information (e.g., "Did you sign the contract?").**
- **Probing Questions**: Encourage elaboration (e.g., "What happened next?"). Probing questions helps uncover information layers that may not surface with initial responses.
- **Clarifying Questions**: These questions ensure comprehension (e.g., "Can you explain that further?"). They are crucial when a client's ambiguous response requires additional detail.

Techniques for Effective Questioning

- **Logical Sequence**: Organize questions to flow from general to specific. Starting with broad questions can help establish context before delving into specifics.
- **Avoiding Leading Questions**: Frame questions neutrally to prevent biasing client responses. For instance, instead of asking, "You didn't feel threatened, did you?" a neutral question would be, "How did you feel in that situation?"
- **Adaptive Approach**: Be flexible and responsive based on the client's answers. The interviewer should be prepared to adjust their questioning strategy based on shared information, allowing for a more natural and informative dialogue.

Challenges in Questioning

- **Overly Rigid Structures**: Following a strict question format can inhibit the flow of conversation and prevent essential topics from being explored.
- **Client Hesitation**: Some clients may be reluctant to share information, necessitating more skilful questioning techniques to elicit responses.

Gathering Information

Importance of Information Gathering

Collecting accurate and relevant information is essential for effective legal representation and compliance with statutory requirements. Information is the backbone for legal arguments, case strategies, and compliance with legal standards.

Methods of Gathering Information

- **Direct Observation**: Assessing the client's demeanor and emotional responses during the interview. Nonverbal cues can provide valuable insights into a client's state of mind and level of engagement.
- **Documentation Review**: Analyzing contracts, agreements, or previous legal documents related to the case. This review is crucial for verifying claims and understanding the legal framework surrounding the client's situation.
- **Legal Research**: Utilizing legal databases and resources to gather relevant case law and statutes. Staying informed about the latest developments in law can aid lawyers in providing sound advice to clients.

Best Practices for Gathering Information

- **Structured Approach**: Create a checklist or framework to cover all necessary areas. A structured approach ensures that critical topics are not overlooked during the interview.

- **Use of Technology**: Employ recording devices (with consent) or case management software to capture information efficiently. Recording interviews can help lawyers accurately recall details later.
- **Follow-up documentation**: Summarize findings in a written format and confirm with the client for accuracy. Documentation serves as a reference point and can prevent misunderstandings.

Challenges in Information Gathering

- **Inaccurate Information**: Clients may unintentionally provide incorrect information due to memory lapses or misunderstandings.
- **Client Reluctance**: Some clients may hesitate to share sensitive information, which can impact the quality of the data gathered.

Legal Framework and Ethical Considerations

Indian Evidence Act, 1872

The *Indian Evidence Act* outlines principles regarding the admissibility of evidence, which underscores the importance of accurate information gathering. Key provisions include:

- **Section 3**: Defines evidence and its relevance, emphasising the need for evidence to be pertinent to the matter.

- **Section 136**: Discusses the judge's discretion in admitting evidence, highlighting the importance of credibility and reliability in the information presented.

Advocates Act, 1961

This act governs the conduct of lawyers in India. Vital ethical considerations for client interviews include:

- **Section 49**: The Bar Council of India sets rules regarding professional conduct, which lawyers must adhere to during client interactions.
- **Confidentiality**: Lawyers must maintain client confidentiality per the attorney-client privilege principle. This obligation fosters trust and encourages open communication.

Case Law

Several landmark judgments emphasise the importance of proper interviewing techniques in legal practice:

- **K.K. Verma v. Union of India** (AIR 1954 SC 359) Highlighted the necessity of comprehensive understanding in legal representation, reinforcing that lawyers must grasp all nuances of a case to serve their clients effectively.
- **S. P. Chengalvaraya Naidu v. Jagannath** (1994) 1 SCC 1: Stressed the importance of accurate representation of facts in legal proceedings, showcasing the consequences

of poor information gathering.

Ethical Dilemmas

- **Confidentiality vs. Disclosure**: Lawyers may face situations where client confidentiality conflicts with the need to disclose information for ethical reasons. Understanding when and how to navigate these dilemmas is crucial.
- **Balancing Client Interests**: Lawyers must ensure that their actions and advice align with the client's best interests while adhering to legal standards and ethical guidelines.

Challenges in Client Interviews

Cultural and Societal Factors

India is a diverse country with many languages, cultures, and social norms. These factors can significantly influence client interactions. Understanding cultural contexts is crucial for effective communication and avoiding misinterpretations.

Emotional Barriers

Clients may come to interviews with emotional baggage, whether from stressful legal situations or personal issues. Lawyers must be equipped to handle these emotional barriers, utilising empathetic listening to create a safe environment for clients to share openly.

Language and Communication Barriers

Language can pose a significant challenge, especially in a multilingual society like India. Lawyers may need to use interpreters or bilingual staff to facilitate clear communication. Legal jargon can also confuse clients; lawyers should explain concepts in simple terms.

Technology and Accessibility

As legal services increasingly incorporate technology, clients may have varying levels of comfort and familiarity with digital tools. Lawyers must be sensitive to these differences, ensuring that communication remains accessible.

Enhancing Interview Skills

Training and Development

Continuous professional development is essential for enhancing interviewing skills. Workshops, seminars, and courses on communication skills, negotiation tactics, and emotional intelligence can benefit legal practitioners.

Role-Playing and Simulation

Role-playing exercises can help lawyers practice their interviewing techniques in a controlled environment.

Simulations allow practitioners to receive feedback and refine their skills without the pressure of real-life interactions.

Mentorship and Peer Feedback

Establishing mentorship relationships with experienced lawyers can provide invaluable insights and guidance. Peer feedback can also foster a culture of continuous improvement, allowing lawyers to learn from one another's experiences.

Self-Reflection and Continuous Improvement

Lawyers should engage in self-reflection after client interviews to assess their performance and identify areas for improvement. Maintaining a journal of experiences and insights can facilitate ongoing growth.

Case Studies

Successful Client Interviews

- **Case Study 1**: A lawyer employed active listening and empathetic questioning in a family law case, resulting in a favourable outcome for the client.
- **Case Study 2**: A criminal defence attorney who used strategic questioning techniques to uncover critical evidence, leading to a successful defence.

Lessons Learned from Challenges

- **Case Study 3**: A situation where inadequate information gathering led to a misrepresentation in court, emphasising the need for thoroughness.
- **Case Study 4**: An instance of cultural misunderstandings that resulted in a communication breakdown, highlighting the importance of cultural competence.

Conclusion

Mastering the critical components of client interviews—active listening, strategic questioning, and systematic information gathering—is paramount for legal professionals operating in the Indian legal framework. These skills are not just tools for effective communication but are foundational to the very essence of successful legal practice. A well-executed client interview can have far-reaching implications, influencing the outcome of a case and the quality of the lawyer-client relationship. By honing these skills, legal practitioners can build stronger relationships based on trust, transparency, and mutual respect, essential for effective representation.

Active listening allows lawyers to fully understand the nuances of a client's legal issue, including any unstated concerns or emotions that may affect the case. This deeper level of understanding helps formulate strategies that align with the client's goals and ensures that the lawyer can address potential issues that may not be immediately apparent. On the other hand, the art of questioning—when applied with precision and insight—enables lawyers to extract the most relevant and critical details while at the same time clarifying any ambiguities that could complicate the legal process later on.

Moreover, systematically gathering and organising the information is critical to developing a robust case. Lawyers must not only collect facts but also analyse and structure them in ways that are legally sound and beneficial to their clients. Failure to do so could lead to oversights that weaken legal arguments or compromise the client's position.

Beyond these technical skills, effective client interviewing is deeply intertwined with a lawyer's ethical and professional responsibilities. Adherence to the moral standards set forth by governing bodies, such as the Bar Council of India, is non-negotiable. Lawyers must ensure that they maintain the highest standards of client confidentiality, avoid conflicts of interest, and provide competent representation throughout the case. Therefore, proficiency in interviewing techniques contributes directly to the lawyer's ability to uphold these ethical obligations while delivering high-quality legal service.

As the legal landscape evolves with societal and economic changes, so must the skills and approaches legal professionals use in their client interactions. Lawyers today are expected to navigate an increasingly diverse clientele, where cultural, linguistic, and socio-economic differences may pose unique challenges. Thus, legal practitioners must continuously refine their interviewing techniques to remain relevant and effective in this dynamic environment. By investing in developing these skills, lawyers improve case outcomes and enhance client satisfaction by offering more personalised and responsive legal services.

In conclusion, the importance of mastering the components of client interviews cannot be overstated. Effective listening, questioning, and information gathering form the bedrock of successful legal practice, fostering a transparent and productive working relationship with clients. As client expectations rise and the legal profession grows more complex, lawyers need to adapt, invest in skill development, and understand the unique challenges faced by their clients. Doing so will lead to better legal representation, improved outcomes, and greater client satisfaction, ultimately contributing to the lawyer's success in an ever-evolving legal landscape.

CHAPTER SEVEN

PERCEPTION AND SITUATIONAL ANALYSIS IN LEGAL DECISION MAKING

- Debashish Mohapatra

Abstract

Legal decision-making is a multifaceted process shaped by a complex interplay between perceptional biases, cognitive frameworks, and situational influences. These factors significantly affect how judges, jurors, and other legal actors interpret laws, assess evidence, and render judgments, often challenging the principle of objectivity in legal processes. This paper delves into the psychological and situational dynamics contributing to legal outcomes, drawing from cognitive theories and real-world case studies. The research uncovers these elements' subtle yet profound impact on justice delivery by analysing perceptional biases—such as confirmation and anchoring biases—alongside situational factors like courtroom dynamics, cultural contexts, and media influences. The study highlights the implications of these factors on fairness and the integrity of the legal system, offering actionable recommendations for mitigating bias and promoting objectivity. This paper advocates for reforms in jury instructions, judicial training on implicit bias, and integration of AI-driven tools in legal proceedings to strengthen the objectivity of legal decisions.

INTRODUCTION

Introduction

Legal decision-making is often perceived as a process rooted in objectivity, with outcomes determined by the logical application of legal statutes and precedents. However, the reality of judicial decision-making is far more complex. The decisions made in legal settings, particularly by judges and jurors, are shaped by both conscious and unconscious psychological processes. These processes include cognitive biases, emotional reactions, and perceptional influences, all of which can skew the interpretation of evidence and the application of law. Beyond individual biases, situational factors such as courtroom dynamics, media presence, and social pressures can further shape outcomes.

Understanding the psychological and situational factors influencing legal decision-making is crucial to preserving the justice system's integrity. While professionally trained to be neutral, legal actors are still human beings subject to the same cognitive limitations and emotional influences as the rest of society. Additionally, the legal system operates within the broader societal context, where public perceptions, cultural norms, and media narratives can subtly shape legal processes and outcomes. This research paper explores the various perceptional and situational influences that affect legal decision-making, drawing on both psychological theory and real-world case studies to highlight the complexity of delivering true justice. Finally, it proposes several reforms to mitigate bias and promote greater objectivity within the legal system.

Cognitive Biases in Legal Decision-Making

Confirmation Bias

Confirmation bias is one of the most pervasive and well-documented cognitive biases. It occurs when individuals favour information that supports their preexisting beliefs while disregarding or downplaying information that contradicts them. In legal settings, confirmation bias can significantly impact how evidence is evaluated and interpreted. For example, a juror or judge who initially believes a defendant is guilty may give undue weight to evidence that supports that conclusion while dismissing exculpatory evidence.

The Central Park Five case offers a prominent example of workplace confirmation bias. In this case, five young men of colour were wrongfully convicted of a violent assault mainly based on coerced confessions. The police, prosecutors, and jurors all operated under the assumption that the young men were guilty despite evidence that contradicted this narrative. Once the initial impression of guilt had taken hold, it shaped how subsequent evidence was interpreted, leading to a miscarriage of justice. This case underscores the dangers of confirmation bias in legal decision-making, particularly in high-profile or emotionally charged cases.

Anchoring Bias

Anchoring bias occurs when individuals rely too heavily on the first piece of information they encounter when making decisions. In a legal context, this could manifest as a judge or juror giving disproportionate weight to the first witness testimony or the opening argument of a trial. Even when additional evidence contradicting the initial impression is presented later, the anchor may still exert a powerful influence on decision-making.

For instance, during jury deliberations, if the first witness testifies particularly compellingly, jurors may anchor their opinions on that testimony and discount later evidence that might provide a different perspective. Similarly, opening arguments from attorneys, while not evidence, can create strong anchors in the minds of jurors or judges. Studies have shown that once an anchor is set, it can be difficult for individuals to adjust their thinking, even in the face of new and conflicting information.

Availability Heuristic

The availability heuristic is a mental shortcut that leads people to judge based on the most readily available information rather than considering all relevant data. In legal decision-making, this can cause judges or jurors to give undue weight to highly publicised cases or dramatic pieces of evidence, even if these are not directly relevant to the case at hand.

For example, jurors who have been exposed to extensive media coverage of violent crimes may be more likely to convict in a similar case simply because the images and stories from the media are fresh in their minds. This heuristic can also lead to harsher punishments, as the emotional resonance of high-profile cases can distort perceptions of threat and severity. The availability heuristic demonstrates how external, unrelated factors can influence legal decision-making, leading to outcomes that may not be entirely based on the facts presented during the trial.

Emotional Influences

Emotions play a significant role in shaping legal decisions, often in ways not aligned with legal principles. Research shows that emotions like fear, sympathy, anger, and disgust can all influence how jurors and judges assess evidence and determine the appropriate level of punishment. Fear, for example, may lead to harsher sentencing if a juror or judge perceives a defendant as a significant threat to society. Conversely, sympathy might result in leniency, mainly if the defendant is portrayed as a vulnerable or tragic figure.

In cases involving violent crimes or child victims, emotions like anger or disgust can overwhelm the legal principle of impartiality. This can result in decisions that are more punitive than what the evidence might suggest is warranted. Emotional influences are difficult to eliminate, but acknowledging their presence and educating legal actors about their potential impact is a crucial first step in mitigating their effects.

Stereotyping and Implicit Bias

Implicit bias refers to the subconscious attitudes or stereotypes that individuals hold about certain groups of people. These biases can affect how judges, jurors, and other legal actors perceive defendants, plaintiffs, and witnesses, often without the individual being aware of their influence. In legal contexts, implicit biases related to race, gender, socioeconomic status, and other factors can lead to differential treatment in sentencing, credibility assessments, and jury deliberations.

For example, studies have shown that Black and Latino defendants in the U.S. are more likely to receive harsher sentences than their white counterparts for similar crimes, even when controlling for other factors. This disparity can be partly attributed to implicit biases that associate minority groups with criminality or violence. Implicit bias training for judges and jurors has been proposed to counteract these biases, though the effectiveness of such training remains a subject of debate.

Situational Factors in Legal Decision-Making

Courtroom Dynamics

Courtroom dynamics, including the physical layout of the courtroom, the behaviour of attorneys, and the presence of media, can have a subtle but significant impact on legal decision-making. Research has shown that jurors' seating arrangement, lawyers' demeanour, and even how evidence is presented can influence how judges and jurors perceive the case.

For instance, in high-profile cases with intense media scrutiny, judges and jurors may feel pressure to deliver a verdict that aligns with public opinion. The O.J. Simpson trial and the George Floyd murder trial both serve as examples of how media coverage and public sentiment can shape legal proceedings. In such cases, the desire to avoid controversy or backlash can lead to decisions that are more influenced by external pressures than by the facts of the case.

Groupthink and Jury Deliberations

Groupthink is a psychological phenomenon that occurs when a group's desire for harmony or conformity leads to irrational or dysfunctional decision-making. In the context of a jury, groupthink can result in verdicts that are not based on a careful evaluation of the evidence but rather on the influence of dominant personalities or the majority opinion.

Juries, particularly in lengthy and complex trials, may feel pressured to reach a consensus quickly. In such situations, jurors who hold dissenting opinions may suppress their views in favour of group harmony. This can lead to rushed or poorly considered verdicts, especially in cases where the evidence is ambiguous or contradictory. Jury reforms, such as appointing a neutral facilitator or introducing anonymous polling during deliberations, have been proposed to mitigate groupthink's effects.

Cultural and Social Contexts

Legal systems do not operate in a vacuum; they are deeply embedded in the cultural and social environments of the societies they serve. Cultural norms and social attitudes can influence how laws are interpreted and applied, often in ways legal actors do not explicitly recognise. For example, societal views on gender roles can affect the outcomes of family law cases, with mothers usually favoured in custody battles based on outdated stereotypes about caregiving.

Similarly, racial attitudes can influence criminal sentencing, with minority defendants frequently receiving harsher penalties for similar offences compared to their white counterparts. These disparities highlight the need for greater awareness of how cultural and social contexts shape legal decision-making and for reforms aimed at reducing bias and promoting fairness.

Case Studies of Perception and Situational Influences

The Central Park Five

The Central Park Five case is a powerful example of how perceptional biases and public pressure can distort legal decision-making. In 1989, five Black and Latino teenagers were wrongfully convicted of assault and rape based on coerced confessions and a biased public narrative that portrayed them as violent criminals. The media coverage at the time stoked public fear and outrage, creating an atmosphere in which the boys were presumed guilty before their trial even began.

Confirmation bias played a significant role in the case, as law enforcement officials and prosecutors ignored evidence that contradicted their initial assumptions of guilt. The case outcome was shaped not by the facts but by a combination of public pressure, media influence, and entrenched racial stereotypes. The eventual exoneration of the Central Park Five, years after their wrongful convictions, underscores the dangers of allowing perceptional biases to go unchecked in legal proceedings.

The George Floyd Murder Trial

The trial of Derek Chauvin for the murder of George Floyd in 2020 was conducted under extraordinary situational pressures, including widespread public protests and intense media coverage. While the legal evidence against Chauvin was strong, the broader social environment surrounding the trial raised questions about how external factors influenced the proceedings.

The social and political context of the trial created a situation in which the legal system was under immense pressure to deliver a conviction. While Chauvin's conviction was widely seen as a just outcome, the case illustrates the challenge of maintaining impartiality in high-profile instances where situational influences are most pronounced. It also highlights the need for the legal system to find ways to balance public sentiment with the impartial application of the law.

Mitigating Perceptional and Situational Bias

Given the profound impact of perceptional and situational factors on legal decision-making, several strategies have been proposed to mitigate these influences and promote greater fairness in the legal system.

Jury Instructions and Deliberation Reforms

Judges can play a crucial role in reducing bias by providing precise and thorough instructions to jurors about the dangers of cognitive biases and the importance of focusing solely on the evidence presented. Jury instructions that explicitly warn against common biases, such as confirmation bias and the availability heuristic, can help jurors become more aware of their thought processes.

In addition, reforms to the structure of jury deliberations—such as appointing a neutral facilitator, extending deliberation time, or introducing anonymous polling—can help reduce the influence of groupthink and ensure that decisions are based on a careful evaluation of the evidence rather than social pressures within the group.

Judicial Training on Implicit Bias

Training programs aimed at helping judges recognise and counteract their implicit biases can also be instrumental in promoting fairness. These programs often involve educating judges about the psychological mechanisms behind biases and providing them with strategies for mitigating their effects in the courtroom.

Studies have shown that when judges are made aware of their implicit biases, they are more likely to take steps to ensure that their decisions are objective and based on the law. Therefore, judicial training on implicit bias represents an important step toward creating a more equitable legal system.

Use of Technology in Legal Proceedings

Integrating technology, particularly AI-driven legal tools, offers another promising avenue for reducing bias in legal decision-making. AI can provide an objective analysis of evidence, free from the cognitive biases and emotional influences that affect human decision-makers. For example, AI systems can help judges and lawyers analyse case law and precedents more systematically, ensuring that decisions are grounded in legal standards rather than personal biases.

While AI is not without its challenges—such as concerns about transparency and accountability—it can be a valuable counterbalance to the subjective nature of human decision-making.

Conclusion

Legal decision-making is influenced by a complex web of perceptional and situational factors, from cognitive biases like confirmation and anchoring biases to situational pressures such as media influence and public opinion. If left unchecked, these factors can undermine the objectivity and fairness of the legal process. Through a deeper understanding of these influences, legal actors can take steps to mitigate their effects and promote more impartial decision-making.

By implementing reforms such as more explicit jury instructions, judicial training on implicit bias, and AI tools, the legal system can move closer to its ideal of delivering fair and objective justice. Ultimately, recognising and addressing the human factors that shape legal decision-making is essential to preserving the integrity of the legal system and ensuring that justice is served.

CHAPTER EIGHT

ATTITUDE IN LAW: ITS IMPORTANCE IN CLIENT AND COURTROOM INTERACTIONS

- Rishika Pal

Abstract

Attitude in the legal profession is a significant yet unacknowledged factor affecting legal professionals, their clients, and the courtroom scenario.

This study further considers attitude from many angles related to the relationships between lawyers and their clients, particularly in target areas such as trust and rapport building, communication, satisfaction, and further impacts on the cases. Clients' positive attitudes nurture collaborative relationships, which are vital for them to be appreciated and understood and critical in rendering legal services to them. On the other hand, a negative attitude would lead to poor communication, a lack of trust, and low confidence in the client.

In court, an attorney's demeanour modifies trial judges' impressions, influences advocacy efforts, and shifts jurors' responses. In this discussion paper, the momentary tone of emotion is considered in court proceedings, providing examples that make it obvious how the moods of lawyers can affect judges and juries. In addition, the issues that revolve around attitude and law, especially the law's ethical dimensions, are also examined, focusing on the practitioners' requirements to behave in a manner that safeguards the client's interests and meets legal ethics.

This study reviews the literature and empirical research to demonstrate the significant impact of behaviour on compliance. It suggests that positive behaviour is beneficial and critical to client interaction and success in court.

Finally, this article calls for greater awareness and education about the importance of behaviour in law and advocates for changes in the legal system regarding professionals' responsibility to improve outcomes and overall user experiences.

INTRODUCTION

The legal profession is a social, interactive profession that requires intellectual and interpersonal skills. In this

context, behaviour becomes essential in the formation of relationships between lawyers and their clients and in the interaction of courtroom discussions. Attitude, generally defined as a stable way of thinking about someone or something, affects how lawyers communicate, advocate for, and represent their clients. As client expectations increase and competition rises, the importance of a lawyer's behaviour cannot be ignored. Today, clients receive legal information, support, and advice from their lawyers. Research shows that clients are more likely to choose and be loyal to lawyers with positive attitudes because these attitudes foster trust and cooperation (Katz 2016).
Conversely, bad behaviour can create problems that interfere with effective communication and undermine client trust, leading to legal consequences. Judgment is not just the facts of the case but also the thoughts and feelings of the mind. Lawyers‘ behaviour affects not only their clients but also judges and justices. Lawyers' behaviour influences the judicial process, the defence profession, and the jury, which is an integral part of the trial process. For example, lawyers who are seen as trustworthy and professional are often seen as more credible, thus increasing their ability to inspire. Conversely, those who exhibit hostile or confrontational behaviour may impact decisions in ways that will affect the case outcome.

Negotiation adds another layer of complexity. Legal professionals are bound by ethical standards that require respect, care, and fairness in their interactions with clients and the courts. A lawyer's behaviour can contribute to or undermine these moral obligations. A positive attitude can strengthen a lawyer's commitment to client advocacy, while a negative attitude can undermine ethics or professionalism. Providing general guidance for examining legal implications, this research explores aspects of personality—from their role in building trust and communication to their impact on decision-making and ethical behaviour—demonstrating the need for legal professionals to develop positive attitudes central to their practice.

This article aims to highlight the importance of behaviour in law and advocacy through a detailed review of the literature and religious studies to have more knowledge and education in this area. Finally, positive behaviour not only increases compliance with the law but also helps to promote compassion and general well-being.

Definition and Components of Attitude

The three main parts of attitude are behavioural (actions or propensities to act), affective (feelings and emotions), and cognitive (beliefs and thoughts). These components combine to create a lawyer's overall work style, which affects how they engage with clients, coworkers, and the legal system. Since their actions and communication are filtered through their mental framework, legal professionals' attitudes directly impact how effectively they advocate for their clients. As such, they must know how their attitudes influence their practices.

The Role of Emotional Intelligence

Self-management of oneself and awareness of others' emotions and their management can be defined as emotional intelligence. This applies highly to fields where people often interact, such as law. In this case, a lawyer's emotional intelligence will change how they will likely interact with clients, colleagues, or even the courtroom. For attorneys, high emotional intelligence can be a phenomenal asset. For instance, it helps them deal with the emotional relations among other attorneys, judges, or clients more efficiently. Using these specific skills in their clients' plans directly assists lawyers who appreciate the interdependence of nonverbal and verbal aspects of communication. This also helps persuade the clients to more effectively represent their interests in court in anticipation of the emotional outbursts of clients that may arise during the litigation process. Other than that, empathy—the ability to sense the emotions in the surroundings—sensitive enough to appreciate the effects that aggravate the clients may help solve more than the clients' legal concerns.

On the other hand, lawyers with low emotional intelligence should not expect success in these fields. They may quickly develop difficulties in managing the emotional complications of their clients, such as intervening when a client sobs due to a profound legal understanding.

ROLE OF ATTITUDE IN CLIENT RELATIONSHIPS

Building rapport and Trust

One of the most critical factors in building rapport and trust is the lawyer's attitude toward their client. Clients are susceptible to the demeanour and conduct of their legal counsel because they seek legal advice during stressful, uncertain, and vulnerable periods. Strong lawyer-client relationships are facilitated by an upbeat and sympathetic demeanour, which makes clients feel heard, valued, and supported.

The cognitive aspect of their mindset influences how a lawyer approaches client contact. For instance, a lawyer with a client-centred approach will ensure the client is involved in decision-making, actively listen, and give clear explanations. Conversely, a disinterested or contemptuous approach could cause annoyance and a decline in trust, harming the attorney-client relationship.

Expectations and Client Management

A lawyer's attitude influences how they establish rapport and handle their clients' expectations. When describing the possible outcomes of a case, it is crucial to strike a balance between optimism and realism. While an overly optimistic outlook may create irrational expectations, an excessively pessimistic lawyer may erode the client's trust. A lawyer with emotional intelligence is aware of their tone and demeanour, managing client expectations to preserve trust while educating the client on the reality of the legal process.

The Dimensions of Ethics

The mindset of a lawyer has ethical ramifications as well. As moral standards require, legal practitioners must uphold honesty and integrity while acting in their client's best interests. A careless or haughty lawyer may put success ahead of morality, which could result in acts detrimental to the client or the legal system. On the other hand, an ethical and modest mindset guarantees that the attorney behaves professionally, honouring both the client and the law.

ATTITUDE IN COURTROOM INTERACTIONS

The Lawyers Demeanour and Presentation

A lawyer's demeanour is constantly observed in the courtroom, impacting the opinions of the judge, jury, and opposing counsel. A respectful yet aggressive demeanour is essential for success in the courtroom. While attorneys who seem unsure or hesitant may weaken their case, those who show confidence in their understanding of the law and their client's position have a better chance of persuading the court.

The way lawyers conduct themselves during oral arguments is significant. Emotions—the affective component of attitude—need to be carefully controlled. For instance, a calm, collected, and logical manner communicates professionalism and control, but an excessively emotional or confrontational appearance can turn off jurors or judges. Attorneys must carefully balance respect for courtroom etiquette and enthusiasm for their client's causes.

Interaction with Judges and Opposition

A lawyer's attitude also affects how they engage with the judge and opposing lawyers. Judges are more inclined to see a lawyer who is cooperative and respectful of the court as credible and trustworthy, which can improve results and foster a positive professional image. Conversely, an aggressive or dismissive demeanour can harm a lawyer's reputation and undermine their argument.

A lawyer's demeanour during meetings with opposing lawyers might help or hinder fruitful discussions. Strong client advocacy is vital, but taking too combative a stance can intensify disputes and lower the likelihood of a successful settlement. An attorney who exhibits emotional intelligence and maintains composure and professionalism in the face of animosity is more likely to keep control of the case.

Credibility and Persuasion

A lawyer's capacity to influence the court determines whether a legal argument succeeds. In this process, credibility is crucial, and a lawyer's attitude is essential to building credibility. Credible advocates are more likely to be seen as confident, courteous, and well-prepared attorneys, which raises the possibility that their arguments will be accepted. However, conceit, overconfidence, or a lack of preparation can damage credibility and harm the case's outcome.

CONSEQUENCES OF NEGATIVE ATTITUDES IN LEGAL PRACTICE

Neglecting Customer Satisfaction and Trust

The client and attorney relationship is built on trust, and the attorney's behaviour plays a significant role in establishing and maintaining that trust. When an attorney exhibits negative behaviour (ignorance, denial, or lack of understanding), the client may feel undervalued, unimportant, or misunderstood. This can cause clients to lose confidence in the attorney's ability to represent them effectively, even if they have the necessary legal knowledge. Surprises can make the client feel left out. Regardless of the outcome of the legal issue, this creates a lack of trust and can lead to dissatisfaction with the attorney's service. Clients who feel their attorney is disqualified are less likely to follow legal advice, which can lead to problems. Over time, a reputation for poor customer service can erode an attorney's credibility, potentially costing them referrals and future business. In the increasingly competitive legal industry, negative client experiences can spread quickly through word of mouth or online reviews, negatively impacting an attorney's practice.

Poor Courtroom Performance and Professional Integrity

The behaviour of lawyers in court affects not only their case but also how the judge, jury, and opposing counsel view them. A lawyer who is aggressive, negligent, or overly adversarial can damage their reputation and undermine their case. Judges are less likely to respond favourably to hostile, belligerent, or uncooperative lawyers, which can lead to an adverse decision or environment in court. If a lawyer appears arrogant, impatient, or condescending, jurors will be biased against them, making it harder for them to persuade jurors of their client's position. Similarly, opposing counsel can use a lawyer's bad behaviour to undermine their credibility. In a legal battle, an attorney's reputation for professionalism and respectability is often reflected in the strength of their arguments.

Reduced Ability to Bring in and Retain Clients

Finally, a lawyer's attitude influences their ability to attract and retain clients. The legal profession is highly competitive, and clients are increasingly seeking attorneys who provide expertise and display professionalism, compassion, and clear communication. Lawyers who exhibit a poor attitude during client consultations or meetings are less likely to make a good impression, which might lead to fewer new client inquiries.

Furthermore, bad attitudes can lead to the loss of current clientele. Clients can end their connection with a lawyer if they feel mistreated, disregarded, or insulted, especially in emotionally sensitive matters like family law, criminal defence, or personal injury. When trust is destroyed, it can be difficult for a lawyer to recover the client's faith, and losing even a few clients can have a significant financial impact on a law firm or solo practitioner.

CONCLUSION

Attitude is a crucial component of legal practice. It affects client interactions and the outcome of court cases. To manage expectations, establish trust with clients, and make strong arguments in court, attorneys must develop self-awareness, emotional intelligence, and a positive professional attitude. In one-on-one meetings with clients and public courtroom appearances, a lawyer's credibility and efficacy are influenced by their mannerisms, communication style, and emotional regulation.

The significance of attitude cannot be overstated, even though technical abilities and legal knowledge are essential to a lawyer's success. In addition to strengthening their bonds with clients and coworkers, attorneys can improve their chances of winning in court by adopting the proper mindset. Through professionalism, empathy, and emotional intelligence, legal professionals can navigate the complex interpersonal dynamics of the legal system and better serve their clients.

CHAPTER NINE

LEADERSHIP IN THE LEGAL PROFESSION: CHARACTERISTICS AND THEORIES

- Devansh Sharma

Introduction

This essay examines leadership in the legal field, with an emphasis on key leadership traits and the application of leadership theories. Legal leadership is unique because of the profession's complex interactions, high-stakes decision-making, and ethical requirements. This study assesses how attorneys and other legal professionals handle leadership duties by examining important leadership characteristics and well-known theories such as transformational, servant, and transactional leadership.

Leadership in the legal profession is essential for law firms, legal departments, and larger court systems to operate effectively. Unlike many other businesses, the legal profession's fundamental obligations to justice, ethics, and public service present unique leadership challenges. Legal executives, whether heads of public legal institutions, managing partners, or in-house counsel, must balance their teams' expectations, client requests, and the general requirement to enforce the law.

Legal leadership involves directing people and organisations toward results consistent with moral norms and legal principles, not merely overseeing a group of attorneys or making money. Legal professionals must make difficult decisions, often in hostile environments, while upholding their dedication to justice and equity. A comprehensive awareness of how the legal field evolves, particularly regarding globalisation, technology, and regulatory changes, is also crucial for legal leadership.

Successful legal leadership requires technical proficiency in legal issues and soft skills such as communication, emotional intelligence, and motivation. In addition to the intellectual rigour demanded by the profession, legal leaders must manage the interpersonal dynamics of leading teams through challenging and often stressful situations.

Leadership dramatically influences the culture of legal practice, which extends beyond internal organisational management. Strong legal leaders set the tone for the profession, shaping their organisation's moral principles, inclusivity, and diversity. They profoundly impact the legal system's ability to serve clients and society, creating environments encouraging ethical decision-making, continuous education, and collaboration.

Overview

In the legal sense, leadership refers to directing individuals, groups, or organisations toward morally and legally acceptable results. Leadership is crucial in law because it affects judicial systems, ethical standards, organisational performance, and client interactions. This paper explores leadership theories and traits relevant to the legal field, highlighting its potential and challenges.

Crucial Qualities of Effective Leadership in the Legal Field

Integrity in Ethics

Legal leaders must enforce the law and ethical standards to ensure justice and fairness, with ethics supporting client representation and decision-making.

Analytical Thinking and Decisiveness

Lawyers often face situations requiring quick decisions with significant consequences. Legal leaders must balance logical thinking with risk assessment in managing complex legal matters or business mergers.

Persuasion and Communication

Effective communication in writing and spoken arguments is essential in legal leadership. This skill is demonstrated in negotiation, trial work, and team management.

Emotional Intelligence

Lawyers must manage their own emotions and understand those of others. Emotional intelligence is critical in maintaining professional relationships, particularly in high-stress settings.

Stress Management and Resilience

High-pressure situations, such as strict deadlines and hostile environments, characterise the legal profession. Managing stress for oneself and the team is crucial for effective leadership.

Strategic Thinking and Vision

Influential legal executives are strategic thinkers who can foresee shifts in the law and market trends. Visionary leadership directs pro bono projects, grows practice areas, and establishes the culture of legal firms.

Leadership Theories and Their Application in the Legal Field

Several leadership theories can be adapted to address the specific challenges of legal leadership.

Transformational Leadership

Transformational leaders inspire and motivate their teams by establishing a shared vision and encouraging innovation. This can involve fostering teamwork, encouraging partners to take on leadership roles in legal firms, and motivating younger attorneys.

Transactional Leadership

Transactional leadership relies on rewards and penalties to ensure performance and compliance. This is evident in legal firms, where performance-based systems manage associates and junior attorneys.

Servant Leadership

Servant leaders prioritise the needs of others, focusing on moral leadership, empathy, and volunteerism. This can be seen in pro bono work, client-centred services, and mentorship in the legal profession.

Situational Leadership

Leaders adapt their style based on the team's or individual's needs. In the legal profession, situational leadership involves modifying approaches depending on the complexity of cases or the experience level of team members.

Charismatic Leadership

Charismatic leaders influence others through personal charm and assertive communication. In law, charismatic leadership can impact courtroom outcomes and public opinion, but if it is not balanced, it can also lead to overconfidence or unethical behaviour.

Adaptive Leadership

Adaptive leadership emphasises the ability to inspire individuals and organisations to adjust to changing circumstances. This is essential in the legal profession, especially with technological shifts, globalisation, and regulation.

Leadership Challenges in the Legal Field

Balancing Objectivity and Advocacy

Lawyers must zealously advocate for their clients while maintaining objectivity. Effective leadership requires balancing passionate advocacy with logical dispassion for sound legal decisions.

Ethical Dilemmas

Legal leaders face ethical challenges, such as maintaining confidentiality, avoiding conflicts of interest, and ensuring adherence to legal ethical standards.

Diversity and Gender Issues

The legal profession has historically underrepresented minorities, with leadership roles often dominated by men. Diverse leadership affects decision-making, client relations, and firm culture.

Resistance to Change

Law firms and the legal profession often resist changes in technology, practice, and client expectations. Leaders must foster flexible, progressive processes and overcome resistance to innovation.

Work-Life Balance

The demanding nature of the legal profession, especially in leadership roles, frequently leads to burnout and mental health concerns. Legal leaders play a crucial role in promoting work-life balance for their teams.

The Future of Leadership in the Legal Profession

The Impact of Technology

Advancements in automation, legal technology, and artificial intelligence will continue to challenge traditional leadership structures in the legal profession.

Leadership Development Programs

There is an increasing demand for specialised programs, such as seminars, formal training, and mentorship, to help legal professionals strengthen their leadership skills.

Ethical Leadership in a Globalized World

As legal matters become more interconnected globally, legal leaders must navigate varying ethical standards and cultural expectations while upholding professional integrity.

Conclusion

Leadership in the legal profession requires navigating the complex relationship between law, ethics, and public service. Legal leaders must balance client expectations, team management, and the core values of justice. Effective leadership in this field requires a unique combination of technical expertise, emotional intelligence, strategic vision, and flexibility. Legal leaders influence the culture of their organisations, promote inclusion and diversity, and prepare their teams for the challenges posed by an evolving legal landscape. Strong leadership in the legal profession ultimately contributes to the effectiveness and trustworthiness of the legal system.

CHAPTER TEN

DEVELOPING A POSITIVE ATTITUDE IN LEGAL PRACTICE

- Naina Agarwalla

Abstract

There are common associations with legal practice that, once undertaken, a practitioner becomes stressed, engages in burnout, and encounters moral issues, thus perpetuating negative attitudes towards legal practice. Practitioners, educationists, employers, and other workplace stakeholders increasingly appreciate that individual practitioners should assume positive emotion management as key in ensuring personal health, professional achievement, and sociomoral behaviour while practising the legal profession. By examining psychological perspectives such as Social Learning Theory,

Cognitive-Behavioral Theory, and Growth Mindset Theory, this study will highlight the relevance of a positive attitude among legal practitioners. The literature review brings to the fore some positive effects of positivity on practitioners, including enhanced problem-solving, creativity, and resilience, which are very important in legal practice. The paper also portrays the forces lawyers contend with, including stress, lack of balance between work and family, and moral fatigue, which hinder a positive outlook. Fostering positivity through emotional intelligence initiatives, mentorship, and robust workplace cultures are also considered. In the end, a positive attitude not only enhances the business side of the profession but ensures that lawyers are ethical and satisfied with their careers in the long term. This paper explores the significance of developing a positive attitude within the legal profession, an area often neglected but crucial for long-term success and satisfaction. It examines the intersection of psychology, law, and professional ethics, aiming to provide both theoretical and practical insights. Using a multidisciplinary approach, this research highlights strategies for fostering positivity in high-pressure legal environments, identifies barriers, and evaluates the role of law schools, firms, and individual initiatives in promoting a constructive mindset.

INTRODUCTION

The legal profession is often associated with high levels of stress, intense workloads, and frequent exposure to conflict, all of which can take a toll on a lawyer's mental well-being and outlook. While legal education typically focuses on technical expertise and the mastery of legal theory, the emotional and psychological aspects of lawyering are often overlooked. Yet, the ability to maintain a positive attitude in the face of these challenges is crucial not only for personal well-being but also for professional success.

A positive attitude in legal practice refers to an optimistic, resilient, and constructive mindset that influences how lawyers approach their work, interact with clients, and deal with adversity. It covers staying solution-focused, maintaining ethical standards, and handling stress even in the most demanding professional situations. In conflict-ridden and competitive environments, cultivating this mindset is essential to maintain job satisfaction and performance. The value of the relationship in legal practice cannot be reassessed. Lawyers with a positive attitude are more likely to build a more sustainable relationship with customers, agree on the best results, and approach their work objectively. In addition, with the ability to recover mentally and with growth status, growth experts can navigate the complexity of occupation without pressure. A positive attitude also contributes to ethical decisions—creating lawyers and promoting honesty and fairness in law practice.

Nevertheless, maintaining a positive attitude in the legal field does not cause any problems. Frequent impacts of a high-pressure environment, long-term working hours, and hostile situations can lead to burnout syndrome, stress, and negativity. Law firms and institutions often prioritise the bottom line over employee well-being, which exacerbates these issues, so lawyers must proactively develop stress management strategies, build resilience, and establish support networks that encourage positivity. This article explores the importance of creating a positive attitude in law practice, the obstacles lawyers face in maintaining such an attitude, and strategies to help lawyers succeed despite challenges. This study provides practical insights for lawyers and legal institutions based on psychological theory, professional development strategies, and real-world case studies. In the end, promoting a positive attitude is for personal well-being and creating a more effective, ethical, and compassionate legal practice.

CONCEPTUAL FRAMEWORK

The conceptual framework for developing a positive attitude in legal practice is grounded in psychological theories of attitude formation, the role of mindset in professional development, and the unique pressures legal professionals face. This framework seeks to explain how a positive attitude can be cultivated, the factors influencing it, and its impact on legal practice. A positive attitude is an optimistic and constructive state of mind characterised by resilience, self-confidence, and adaptability. In legal practice, this is reflected in a lawyer's ability to approach work with enthusiasm, perseverance, and solution-oriented thinking, even under stressful or adverse circumstances. A positive attitude includes effectively managing emotional reactions, focusing on long-term goals, and remaining professional even under challenging situations.

In a legal context, this doesn't just mean focusing on the technical aspects of a case but also empathising with clients, collaborating with colleagues, and making ethical decisions. This leads to greater job satisfaction, moral integrity, and client relationships.

Law practice is inherently demanding as it involves interpreting and applying complex laws in an adversarial system. Whether in litigation, corporate or public interest law, lawyers face tight deadlines, high-stakes cases, and the need to balance competing interests. Many legal systems' adversarial nature, client demands, and the need to achieve positive outcomes can contribute to stress and burnout. This profession also heavily emphasises results and performance, often at the expense of work-life balance, leading to burnout. In such environments, a lawyer's attitude becomes crucial in maintaining mental well-being, managing professional relationships, and ensuring ethical practices. The concept of thinking, especially the theory of growth, compared to the fixed thinking developed by psychologist Carol Dweck, plays a vital role in forming lawyers' attitudes. The increase reflects the belief that abilities and intelligence can be developed through effort and training. In contrast, a fixed mindset assumes abilities are static, which can lead to a defeatist attitude when problems arise.

Lawyers with a growth mindset are more likely to view obstacles as opportunities for learning and personal growth in the legal profession. They are open to feedback, seek continuous improvement, and embrace the evolving nature of law and legal practice. Conversely, those with a fixed mindset may see challenges as threats, leading to frustration, apathy, and negative attitudes. A conceptual framework for cultivating a positive attitude in legal practice integrates psychological theory, professional challenges, and practical solutions. Legal professionals can improve their performance, career happiness, and satisfaction by cultivating emotional intelligence, resilience, and a growth mindset.

Overcoming barriers such as stress, competition, and work-life imbalance requires a proactive approach, but the benefits of a positive attitude in the legal profession are far-reaching. A positive attitude improves client outcomes, ethical decision-making, and a more sustainable career trajectory.

LITERATURE REVIEW

The literature on developing positive attitudes in legal practice highlights the importance of maintaining a constructive mindset in a profession characterised by high-stress levels and conflicting challenges. Various psychological frameworks, such as social learning theory, cognitive behavioural theory, and growth mindset theory, offer insight into how lawyers can cultivate positivity. Social learning theory posits that lawyers, especially junior practitioners, learn from more experienced colleagues to adapt their attitudes and behaviours. Thus, a positive, uplifting work environment promotes optimism. Cognitive behavioural theory explains how lawyers can counter the all-or-nothing or catastrophic negative thinking patterns common in high-pressure professions. Adopting a growth mindset, as described by Carol Dweck, allows lawyers to view challenges as opportunities for growth rather than obstacles, promoting resilience.

Empirical research highlights the benefits of a positive attitude in the legal profession, including enhanced problem-solving abilities, creativity, and emotional intelligence. A positive attitude also supports ethical decision-making, as lawyers who maintain an optimistic attitude can better deal with complex ethical dilemmas without getting frustrated. However, serious issues such as burnout, work-life imbalance, and moral exhaustion often impede the development of a positive outlook on legal practice. These issues lead to cynicism and alienation, affecting job satisfaction and work ethic. Strategies to overcome these barriers include mindfulness, self-awareness, mentoring, and creating a supportive work culture. By developing emotional intelligence and adopting a growth mindset, lawyers can build and maintain a positive attitude that enhances their well-being and professional effectiveness.

The literature on cultivating positive attitudes in legal practice highlights the critical role that attitudes, emotional intelligence, and professional support play in shaping lawyers' approach to their work. Although the legal profession is inherently demanding, with high-stress levels, ethical dilemmas, and workload pressures, lawyers with a positive attitude are better equipped to overcome these challenges and achieve long-term success. Theoretical frameworks such as social learning theory, cognitive behavioural theory, and growth mindset theory provide valuable insights into how attitudes are formed and maintained in the legal profession. Experienced research emphasises the benefits of positivity, from advanced abilities to solving problems for clients and improving ethical solutions.

At the same time, the literature also recognises significant barriers facing legal experts, such as burnout, imbalances in labour life, and moral fatigue. To overcome these challenges, lawyers must develop strategies to manage stress, increase resilience, and build professional support networks. Law firms and institutions are also responsible for creating an environment that encourages a positive attitude, resulting in better outcomes for lawyers and clients.

IMPORTANCE AND CHALLENGES IN DEVELOPING A POSITIVE ATTITUDE IN LEGAL PRACTICE

Developing a positive attitude in legal practice is crucial for several reasons. A positive attitude has significantly impacted job performance, interpersonal relationships, and ethical decision-making in various professional fields, including law. Positive psychology, led by researchers such as Martin Seligman, highlights the benefits of optimism, resilience, and emotional intelligence in career success. These qualities are essential in the stressful and conflict-ridden practice of law.

For instance, a positive attitude enhances problem-solving abilities and creativity. Barbara Fredrickson's broaden-and-build theory argues that positive emotions expand cognitive processes, enabling individuals to think more broadly and develop innovative solutions. Lawyers with positive attitudes are more likely to approach complex cases creatively and flexibly, leading to better client outcomes.

Moreover, studies in emotional intelligence (EI) suggest that lawyers with higher emotional intelligence are better equipped to manage stress, build strong client relationships, and maintain professional composure in high-pressure situations. Krieger and Sheldon's (2015) study on well-being in the legal profession found that lawyers who reported higher levels of autonomy, purpose, and optimism experienced greater job satisfaction and professional fulfilment. Emotional intelligence enables lawyers to maintain empathy and ethical standards, even when faced with adversarial situations, ultimately contributing to a more ethical law practice.

Despite the clear advantages of a positive attitude, lawyers face many problems maintaining such thoughts. Burnout syndrome is one of the most critical issues for legal professionals. The Journal of the American Bar Association (ABA) (2018) reports that many lawyers experience high levels of stress, anxiety, and depression, mainly due to heavy workloads, client pressure, and the hostile nature of the profession. Burnout often leads to cynicism, alienation, and negative attitudes, harming professional performance and personal well-being. Work-life imbalance is another crucial factor contributing to lawyers' negative attitudes. Schiltz (1999) observed that the demanding nature of legal work, especially in large law firms, often results in overtime, interpersonal tensions, and a reduced quality of life. This imbalance contributes to disappointment and fatigue, making it difficult for lawyers to maintain positive views of their work and life.

In addition, lawyers often face ethical dilemmas, which can lead to moral fatigue. Rest's (1986) model of moral decision-making suggests that repeatedly making difficult moral decisions without sufficient emotional and professional support can undermine a lawyer's ethical resolve. Over time, this can contribute to developing negative attitudes toward the profession and increase the risk of unethical behaviour. Lawyers who lack the emotional stability to navigate these dilemmas can be disappointed with their work, further strengthening negative relationships.

CONCLUSION

This research paper addresses lawyers' unique challenges and explores the importance of cultivating a positive attitude in the legal profession and the benefits of cultivating a constructive mindset. The introductory chapter discusses common issues such as stress, burnout, and ethical dilemmas in legal practice, highlighting the need to cultivate positivity to improve well-being and professional performance. The study's conceptual framework is based on psychological theories such as social learning theory, cognitive behavioural theory (CBT), and growth mindset theory. These basic principles show how attitudes are formed and how lawyers can change negative thinking patterns into positive ones. The literature review provides empirical evidence supporting the benefits of a positive attitude, including improved problem-solving skills, creativity, emotional intelligence, and ethical decision-making.

Despite these benefits, lawyers face many obstacles to developing a positive attitude, including burnout, work-life imbalance, and mental exhaustion. These challenges can lead to cynicism and disengagement, impacting personal well-being and professional ethics. The paper emphasises the importance of implementing mindfulness, self-awareness, mentorship, and supportive workplace cultures to overcome these barriers. In conclusion, this article argues that cultivating a positive attitude is essential for personal growth and professional success in the legal field. By prioritising the positive, lawyers can increase their resilience, improve client relationships, and promote ethical practice, thereby contributing to a healthier legal environment and a more efficient justice system.

www.ingramcontent.com/pod-product-compliance
Lightning Source LLC
La Vergne TN
LVHW041035150826
845672LV00001B/329